THE ONE YEAR DEVOTIONAL FOR COUPLES

5-MINUTE DEVOTIONS & PRAYERS TO DEEPEN YOUR RELATIONSHIP, STRENGTHEN COMMUNICATION, AND GROW CLOSER TO GOD — FOR A MORE INTIMATE CONNECTION

BIBLICAL TEACHINGS

Copyright © 2025 by Biblical Teachings - All rights reserved.

No part of this book may be reproduced in any form or by any electronic or mechanical means, including information storage and retrieval systems, without written permission from the author, except for the use of brief quotations in a book review.

Under no circumstances will any blame or legal responsibility be held against the publisher, or author, for any damages, reparation, or monetary loss due to the information contained within this book, either directly or indirectly.

Legal Notice:

This book is copyright protected. It is only for personal use. You cannot amend, distribute, sell, use, quote, or paraphrase any part, or the content within this book, without the author or publisher's permission.

Disclaimer Notice:

Please note that the information contained within this document is for educational and entertainment purposes only. All effort has been executed to present accurate, up-to-date, reliable, complete information. No warranties of any kind are declared or implied. Readers acknowledge that the author is not rendering legal, financial, medical, or professional advice. The content within this book has been derived from various sources. Please consult a licensed professional before attempting any techniques outlined in this book.

By reading this document, the reader agrees that under no circumstances is the author responsible for any losses, direct or indirect, that are incurred due to the use of the information in this document, including, but not limited to, errors, omissions, or inaccuracies.

CONTENTS

Beginning Together   ix

1. Making Time for What Matters Most   1
2. Balancing Life & Faith   3
3. Cutting Out the Clutter   5
4. Encouragement When Life Gets Busy   7
5. Handling Disagreements   12
6. Starting Meaningful Conversations   14
7. Listening Before Speaking   16
8. Learning from Our Wins   18
9. Finding Our Mission as a Couple   22
10. Making Time to Serve Together   24
11. Supporting Each Other's Passions in Service   26
12. Serving in Small Ways Every Day   28
13. Nurturing Emotional Intimacy   32
14. Daily Acts of Appreciation   34
15. Understanding Physical Intimacy   36
16. Balancing Heart & Body   38
17. Setting Boundaries with Family   42
18. Honoring Parents, Prioritizing Marriage   44
19. Creating Family Traditions   46
20. Dealing with Family Stress   48
21. Faith and Finances   52
22. Setting Financial Goals Together   54
23. Making Decisions as a Team   56
24. Praying Over Our Finances   58
25. Intentional Co-Parenting   62
26. Modeling Values for Our Kids   64
      Encourage Others by Sharing Your Experience   66
27. Aligning Our Parenting Approach   68
28. Bringing Faith into Family Time   70
29. Supporting Each Other Through Stress   74
30. Turning to Prayer in Hard Times   76
31. Balancing Individual Needs & Shared Responsibilities   78
32. Identifying & Addressing Stress Triggers   80
33. Celebrating Our Milestones   84
34. Reflecting on Our Growth   86
35. Setting New Goals Together   88

36. Making Gratitude a Habit	90
37. The Role of Forgiveness in Our Marriage	94
38. Extending Grace to Each Other	96
39. Forgiving & Moving Forward Together	98
40. Reminding Each Other of God's Grace	100
41. Staying Consistent in Our Faith	104
42. Keeping Each Other Accountable	106
43. Building Faith-Centered Routines	108
44. Overcoming Obstacles Together	110
45. Encouraging Personal & Spiritual Growth	114
46. Nurturing Each Other's Talents	116
47. Challenging Each Other in Faith	118
48. Pursuing Growth Opportunities Together	120
49. Lessons Learned in Our Marriage	124
50. Envisioning Our Future Together	126
51. Applying God's Wisdom in Our Marriage	128
52. Keeping God at the Center of Our Plans	130
Keeping Your Love Story Alive	134
Continuing Together	137

BIBLE STUDY
-Starter Kit-

Discover a **Simple**, **Powerful** Way to Study **The Bible**

- *No More Guesswork* - Learn to Explore the Bible **with Confidence** and Clarity.

- Discover a Study Method That *Fits Seamlessly into Your Busy Life* - **Without the Overwhelm**.

- **Build a Bible Study Routine** *You'll Actually Look Forward To* - Not Just Another Task on Your To-Do List.

SCAN THE QR CODE FOR YOUR FREE COPY

This journey belongs to...

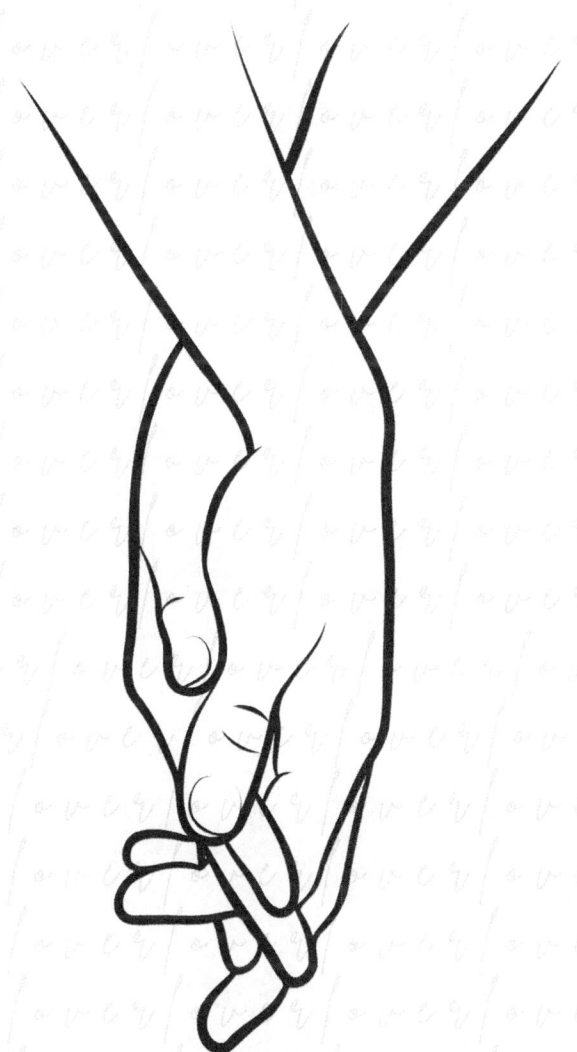

_____   _____

BEGINNING TOGETHER

Welcome to the *One Year Devotional Workbook for Couples*. Life can get busy, and sometimes it feels like there's not enough time to focus on your relationship with your spouse or your faith. This devotional is here to help you carve out that much-needed time to reconnect with each other and grow in your walk with God.

Each section of this devotional is designed to guide you through real-life conversations, reflections, and prayers, all aimed at bringing you and your spouse closer to one another and to God. We've included Bible verses, relatable stories, and simple ideas to help you apply your faith in everyday moments as a couple.

Whether you're just starting your journey together or have been married for years, taking intentional time for each other is always important. Life may not slow down, but this devotional gives you a chance to pause and focus on what matters most—your marriage and your faith.

How to Use This Book:

1. **Go at Your Own Pace:** Every couple is different, so use this devotional in a way that fits your life. You can read through it daily, weekly, or whenever you find the time. The key is to make space for each other, no matter how busy things get.
2. **Start with Scripture:** Each devotion begins with a Bible verse to set the tone and give you a foundation to build on. Let these verses guide your thoughts and conversations.

BEGINNING TOGETHER

3. **Relatable Stories:** After the scripture, you'll find a "Heartfelt Moment"—a real-life story or reflection that speaks to the ups and downs of marriage and faith. Take a few minutes to think about how these stories connect with your own experiences as a couple.
4. **Practical Tips:** In the "Wisdom for the Walk" section, you'll find practical suggestions for growing closer to each other and to God. These tips are simple and easy to work into your daily lives.
5. **Heart-to-Heart Conversations:** Use the conversation starters to talk openly about your relationship, faith, and how you can support each other. These prompts are meant to help you dive deeper into meaningful conversations.
6. **Pray Together:** End each devotional by praying together, asking God to bless your marriage and give you strength as you continue to grow in love and faith.
7. **Workbook Pages:** After every 4 devotions, you'll find a 2-page workbook section designed to help you reflect, journal, and take action based on what you've explored. These come *after* the devotions on purpose — so you can first engage with the content, then process and apply it together. Think of them as guided moments to pause, connect, and grow closer to each other and to God.

This devotional is all about making time for each other in the middle of life's busyness. It's a chance to pause, reflect, and refocus on what really matters—your relationship with God and with each other.

We hope that as you work through these devotions, you'll find new ways to connect, support, and love each other, drawing closer to God and to the beautiful relationship He's given you.

P.S. *All scripture quotations are taken from the Holy Bible, New International Version (NIV), unless otherwise noted.*

1

MAKING TIME FOR WHAT MATTERS MOST

"Be very careful, then, how you live—not as unwise but as wise, making the most of every opportunity, because the days are evil."

— EPHESIANS 5:15-16

I'll admit it: life gets busy. Between work, family, and the never-ending list of tasks, it sometimes feels like there's no time left for anything else. But as the years have passed, I've learned that making time for what truly matters—like spending time with God and my spouse—requires more than just good intentions. It requires intentional action.

There was a season when my husband and I barely had time to breathe, let alone sit down for a devotional together. We would go weeks without opening our Bibles, and our prayers were quick and rushed—if they happened at all. We both felt the strain it put on our relationship, but it seemed impossible to find a solution.

That's when we stumbled upon a quote by Stephen Covey: *"The key is not to prioritize what's on your schedule, but to schedule your priorities."* That simple statement turned everything around for us. We realized that time wouldn't magically appear; we had to reclaim it by scheduling what mattered most. So, we made a decision: we would prioritize our devotional time, even if it meant sacrificing something else. Instead of watching TV before bed, we would read a short devotional and pray together.

BIBLICAL TEACHINGS

We started small, with just ten minutes a day, but those ten minutes made all the difference. Over time, those ten minutes turned into fifteen, then twenty, and before we knew it, spending time in God's Word together became a non-negotiable part of our daily routine.

What we learned is that time isn't something you find; it's something you make. By intentionally carving out time for devotionals, we not only grew closer to God but also to each other. And here's the beautiful thing: the more we made time for what mattered, the more time seemed to stretch. We found that God honored our commitment by giving us the strength and energy to manage everything else.

Next Steps

1. **Start Small:** If finding time for a full devotional seems daunting, start with just five or ten minutes a day. Consistency matters more than duration.
2. **Schedule It:** Just like you would schedule a meeting or an appointment, put devotional time on your calendar. Treat it as a non-negotiable commitment.
3. **Eliminate Distractions:** Identify time-wasters in your day—like excessive screen time—and replace them with moments of spiritual connection.

Real Talk

- What are some specific time-wasters in your daily routine that you could replace with devotional time?
- How can you support each other in staying consistent with your devotionals?

Short Prayer

Lord, help us to be wise with our time and to prioritize what truly matters. Give us the discipline to carve out moments for You, no matter how busy life gets. Strengthen our bond as we grow closer to You and to each other. Amen.

2

BALANCING LIFE & FAITH

"Be wise in the way you act toward outsiders; make the most of every opportunity."

— COLOSSIANS 4:5

Balancing life's many demands with your spiritual journey can be a real challenge. With work, family, social events, and even the need to unwind, it's easy for the day to slip away before you've had a moment to connect with your faith.

Consider how we consume media today. For instance, Netflix's autoplay feature makes it effortless to binge-watch an entire series without realizing how much time has passed. Suddenly, the time you intended for quiet reflection is gone, replaced by hours in front of a screen. Just as Netflix gives us a countdown before the next episode begins, we too have moments to pause, reassess, and choose how we spend our time.

It's natural to wonder, *"How can I possibly fit more into my already packed day?"* The key is in making small, intentional changes. Think about the moments you usually spend scrolling through social media or flipping channels. Could you swap just one of those activities for something that feeds your spirit? Perhaps it's reading a chapter from the Bible, listening to a worship song, or simply sitting quietly in prayer for five minutes.

BIBLICAL TEACHINGS

Your free time is a precious opportunity—a chance to draw closer to God and invite His presence into the busyness of life. It doesn't require a major overhaul, just a willingness to weave spiritual practices into your existing routine. These small shifts can add up, deepening your faith and enriching your relationship with each other over time.

Next Steps

1. **Start with Five Minutes:** Dedicate just five minutes of your free time to a spiritual activity. Whether it's reading a devotion, praying together, or reflecting on a scripture verse, those minutes add up.
2. **Incorporate Faith into What You Love:** If you enjoy listening to music, try incorporating worship songs into your playlist. If you're a reader, consider adding a faith-based book to your rotation.
3. **Be Intentional with Downtime:** Instead of automatically turning to the TV or phone, use a portion of your downtime to connect with God, either alone or as a couple.

Real Talk

- How do you currently spend your free time, and where could you make space for more spiritual activities?
- What small changes could you make to ensure that your daily routines include moments to connect with God and each other?

Short Prayer

Lord, help us be mindful of how we spend our time. Guide us to make the most of every opportunity, not just for ourselves but also for our relationship with You and with each other. Teach us to find balance in busyness and to prioritize what truly matters. Amen.

3

CUTTING OUT THE CLUTTER

"Therefore, since we are surrounded by such a great cloud of witnesses, let us throw off everything that hinders and the sin that so easily entangles. And let us run with perseverance the race marked out for us."

— HEBREWS 12:1

Life is full of distractions. Whether it's the constant buzz of notifications, the temptation to binge-watch another episode, or the endless scroll through social media, there's no shortage of things competing for our attention. It's easy to get caught up in the noise and lose sight of what really matters—our relationships, our spiritual growth, and our time with God.

I remember one evening when my husband and I had planned to spend some quiet time together, reflecting on the day and reading a devotional. But before we knew it, we were both glued to our phones, mindlessly scrolling through Instagram and Facebook. An hour passed, and by the time we looked up, it was too late to do anything meaningful. The opportunity for connection had slipped away, replaced by a fog of distractions that left us feeling disconnected and empty.

It made me think of a quote I once read: *"The more you subtract, the more you add."* It's a simple truth, yet so powerful. Cutting out the clutter—those unnecessary distractions—makes room for the things that truly matter. Just as Hebrews 12:1 urges us to *"throw off everything that hinders,"* we realized that if we wanted to prioritize our relationship with each other and with God, we had to make some changes.

So, we took a hard look at our daily routines and identified the biggest time-wasters. For us, it was excessive screen time—social media, TV, and mindless browsing. We made a conscious decision to limit these distractions, setting boundaries around our usage and creating *"unplugged"* time where we focus on each other and on our spiritual growth. It wasn't easy at first, but the results were undeniable. We found that by cutting out the clutter, we made space for deeper conversations, more meaningful devotional time, and a stronger connection with God.

As Marie Kondo says, *"The question of what you want to own is actually the question of how you want to live your life."* Just as decluttering our homes brings joy, decluttering our lives brings peace and spiritual growth.

Next Steps

1. **Identify Your Distractions:** Take note of time-stealers like social media, TV, or other activities that don't add value to your life.
2. **Set Boundaries:** Create limits on how much time you spend on these activities. Consider no-screen zones or times to prioritize face-to-face connection and spiritual practices.
3. **Replace the Clutter with Connection:** Use the reclaimed time to focus on God and each other, through prayer, conversation, or shared activities.

Real Talk

- What are the biggest distractions or time-wasters in your daily life, and how do they impact your relationship with each other and with God?
- What boundaries can you set to reduce these distractions and create more time for meaningful connection and devotionals?

Short Prayer

Lord, help us to identify and remove the distractions that keep us from growing closer to You and to each other. Give us the strength and discipline to focus on what truly matters and to run the race You've set before us with perseverance. Amen.

4

ENCOURAGEMENT WHEN LIFE GETS BUSY

"Therefore encourage one another and build each other up, just as in fact you are doing." 1

— THESSALONIANS 5:11

When life gets hectic, it's easy for devotional time to slip through the cracks. Between work, family, and other responsibilities, finding time to connect with God can be challenging. But this is when encouraging each other becomes really important. Supporting one another in keeping your faith practices alive, even during the busiest seasons, can strengthen both your relationship with each other and with God.

One way to stay on track is by finding a routine that works for both of you. Maybe it's praying together before breakfast, sharing a Bible verse over coffee, or winding down with a short devotional before bed. When you make these moments a natural part of your day, they're easier to stick with—even when life gets busy.

Another helpful approach is gentle reminders. You don't need to nag each other, but a simple, kind reminder can make a big difference. For example, sending a quick text to check in or setting a time to talk about what you've read can help you both stay committed without feeling pressured.

It's also great to encourage each other with positive words. When one of you feels overwhelmed or tired, offering a reminder of how much these spiritual

BIBLICAL TEACHINGS

moments mean can help keep you both motivated. Sometimes, just knowing that your partner appreciates the effort can be enough to keep going.

Lastly, be flexible. If your usual devotional time doesn't work on a particular day, don't stress—just find another time that does. The key is to keep the habit alive, even if it looks a little different each day.

Next Steps

1. **Find a Routine:** Make spiritual practices part of your daily routine. Even small moments can have a big impact.
2. **Gentle Reminders:** Support each other with loving reminders to stay connected to your faith.
3. **Encourage Each Other:** Use positive words to lift each other up, especially when life feels overwhelming.
4. **Stay Flexible:** Adjust your devotional time as needed to fit your schedule. The goal is consistency, not perfection.

Real Talk

- How can we encourage each other to stay committed to our devotional time when life gets busy?
- What small changes can we make to keep our spiritual practices a priority?

Short Prayer

Lord, thank You for giving us each other to walk this journey together. Help us to encourage one another and stay committed to our time with You, even when life gets busy. Guide us as we build habits that keep us close to You and to each other. Amen.

Prioritizing Time Together

Pause & Reflect

Where can we create more space for "us" in our busy schedules?

Plan & Promise

What's one small habit we can commit to this week to make our devotional time together a priority?

Wife

Husband

Create & Connect

Draw a simple timeline of your day and mark where you can spend 10 minutes together for prayer or a devotional.

Time spent together is time invested in love. The moments we carve out for each other are the threads that strengthen the bond between us.

5

HANDLING DISAGREEMENTS

"My dear brothers and sisters, take note of this: Everyone should be quick to listen, slow to speak, and slow to become angry."

— JAMES 1:19

Disagreements are a natural part of any relationship. Whether it's a minor difference of opinion or a heated argument, the way you handle these moments can either bring you closer together or create distance. How you communicate during conflicts significantly influences the outcome.

Think back to the last time you had a disagreement. Did you find yourselves talking over each other, desperate to make your point heard? Or perhaps you avoided the conversation altogether, shutting down instead? These reactions are common, but they often complicate conflict resolution. It's easy to slip into these patterns, especially when emotions are running high.

This brings to mind a scene from the movie *Inside Out*, where the characters representing different emotions argue over how to handle a situation. Each one tries to take control, but the chaos only grows until they learn to work together. Our emotions can be like those characters—each vying for dominance in a conversation. However, when we manage them with patience and grace, navigating disagreements becomes much easier.

Improving communication during disagreements doesn't mean avoiding them; it means approaching them with the right mindset. Next time you're in the middle of a disagreement, remember that the goal isn't to win the argument but to grow together. Focus on listening, being patient, and speaking with love and respect. Over time, handling disagreements with grace will become second nature, strengthening your bond as a couple.

Next Steps

1. **Listen First:** Before responding, make sure you fully understand what your partner is saying. This shows respect and can prevent misunderstandings.
2. **Pause and Reflect:** Take a moment before speaking to ensure your response is measured and not driven by emotion.
3. **Speak with Kindness:** Choose your words carefully, focusing on resolution rather than blame. Remember, it's about finding a solution together.

Real Talk

- How do you typically handle disagreements, and what can you do to improve your communication during conflicts?
- What steps can you take to ensure that you listen more and react with patience during your next disagreement?

Short Prayer

Lord, teach us to be quick to listen, slow to speak, and slow to become angry. Help us to approach disagreements with grace, seeking to understand each other and to communicate with love. Strengthen our relationship as we learn to handle conflicts in a way that honors You. Amen.

6

STARTING MEANINGFUL CONVERSATIONS

"A gentle answer turns away wrath, but a harsh word stirs up anger."

— PROVERBS 15:1

In any relationship, there are times when difficult topics need to be discussed. These conversations can be challenging, but they're also opportunities to deepen your understanding of each other and to grow closer. Over time, I've learned that the key to discussing tough subjects without letting them turn into arguments is to approach each conversation with love, respect, and a genuine desire to understand my partner's perspective.

One effective strategy is choosing the right time and setting. It's best to have these discussions when both of us are calm and not distracted. Setting aside specific time for talking creates a safe space where we can focus on the topic without feeling rushed or stressed.

Starting with open-ended questions can also make a big difference. Instead of diving straight into the issue, I like to begin with questions that invite thoughtful reflection. For example, instead of saying, *"Why didn't you do this?"* I might ask, *"How do you feel about what happened?"* This encourages honest sharing without putting my partner on the defensive.

Using *"I"* statements rather than *"you"* statements is another helpful approach. For example, saying *"I feel concerned about..."* instead of *"You always..."* helps me express my feelings without sounding accusatory. This small shift in language can prevent the conversation from becoming confrontational and keeps the focus on resolving the issue together.

Active listening is key as well. This means truly hearing what my partner is saying rather than waiting for my turn to speak. Repeating back what I've heard or asking clarifying questions shows I'm engaged and value their perspective. This prevents misunderstandings and helps the other person feel respected and heard.

Finally, I remind myself that the goal isn't to "win," but to understand each other better and find a solution that works for both of us. Keeping this in mind helps me stay calm and focused, even when the topic is difficult.

Next Steps

1. **Choose the Right Time and Place:** Have tough conversations when you're both calm and free from distractions, setting a positive tone.
2. **Ask Open-Ended Questions:** Start with questions that invite reflection and understanding, rather than putting the other person on the defensive.
3. **Use "I" Statements:** Focus on expressing your feelings rather than blaming your partner.
4. **Listen Actively:** Show you're engaged by repeating back what you've heard or asking clarifying questions.
5. **Focus on Understanding, Not Winning:** Keep the goal in mind—growing closer, not proving a point.

Real Talk

- What are some conversation starters or questions that can help us discuss difficult topics without arguing?
- How can we create a safe space for discussing tough subjects in our relationship?

Short Prayer

Lord, thank You for the wisdom in Your Word. Help us approach difficult conversations with love, patience, and understanding. Guide us to communicate openly and respectfully, always seeking to grow closer to each other and to You. Amen.

7

LISTENING BEFORE SPEAKING

"To answer before listening—that is folly and shame."

— PROVERBS 18:13

When emotions run high, it's easy to react impulsively without really listening. In the heat of the moment, focusing on your own point can drown out what the other person is saying. But communication isn't just about expressing yourself; it's about truly listening, even when it's challenging.

Take Mike and Lisa, for example. After ten years of marriage, they know each other well, but like any couple, they have their disagreements. One evening, after a particularly stressful day, a small issue quickly escalated into a heated argument. Mike, ready to defend his stance, was more focused on crafting his next response than on hearing Lisa out. Meanwhile, Lisa felt ignored and frustrated. The argument spiraled out of control because neither was genuinely listening.

This scenario reminds me of the film *Before Sunrise*, where Jesse and Celine navigate deep, meaningful conversations that sometimes lead to disagreements. What makes their connection so powerful is their ability to truly listen, even during tough conversations. They understand that listening isn't just about hearing words; it's about grasping the emotions behind them and responding with empathy.

When couples rush to defend themselves or react out of anger without fully understanding their partner's perspective, they risk intensifying the conflict. True communication requires active listening—tuning in not just to the words but also to the feelings behind them. It means pausing, setting aside your own thoughts, and giving your partner the space to express themselves completely.

Mike and Lisa recognized that their arguments often escalated because they weren't truly listening to each other. They decided to practice *"reflective listening,"* where each person repeats back what they heard before responding. This small adjustment made a significant difference, slowing down their conversations and ensuring that both felt heard, even during disagreements.

Next Steps

1. **Pause Before Responding:** When emotions are high, take a moment to breathe before you respond. This allows you to calm down and focus on what's being said.
2. **Reflect What You Hear:** Practice reflective listening by repeating back what your partner says to ensure you've understood them correctly. This also shows that you're fully engaged in the conversation.
3. **Empathize and Validate:** Acknowledge your partner's feelings, even if you don't agree with their perspective. Validation helps to defuse tension and create a more constructive dialogue.

Real Talk

- How can you practice active listening, especially when you're upset with each other?
- What are some techniques you can use to ensure you truly understand each other's viewpoints before responding?

Short Prayer

Lord, help us to be quick to listen and slow to speak, especially in moments of conflict. Teach us to hear each other's hearts and to respond with love and understanding. Guide us in building a relationship that honors You through our words and actions. Amen.

8

LEARNING FROM OUR WINS

"Be kind and compassionate to one another, forgiving each other, just as in Christ God forgave you."

— EPHESIANS 4:32

Conflict is a natural part of any relationship, but the way we handle it can make all the difference. There's something deeply satisfying about reflecting on a conflict that was resolved well—knowing that, even in a tough situation, we navigated it with grace, understanding, and love. It serves as a reminder that with God's guidance, we can overcome challenges together.

One of the most memorable conflicts my spouse and I resolved stemmed from a misunderstanding about how we were spending our free time. We both felt neglected but didn't address it directly, allowing our frustrations to build beneath the surface. Eventually, it came to a head one evening, and we realized it was time for an honest conversation.

What made that resolution effective was our decision to approach the conversation with empathy instead of defensiveness. I remember thinking about a scene from the movie *The Vow*, where the couple struggles to reconnect after a traumatic event. At one point, they realize that moving forward requires truly understanding each other's feelings, even when it's difficult. This shift in focus—from trying to be right to striving to understand—helped us see the situation from each other's perspective.

In that moment, we chose kindness over pride and compassion over resentment. We acknowledged the hurt we had caused each other and, instead of dwelling on past mistakes, concentrated on finding a path forward together.

Looking back, I realize that our ability to resolve that conflict was rooted in our willingness to forgive and let go. We didn't let the issue fester; instead, we confronted it head-on with a shared commitment to growing stronger as a couple. It wasn't easy, but it was worth it. The resolution not only strengthened our relationship but also taught us the power of humility, compassion, and forgiveness.

Next Steps

1. **Prioritize Empathy:** When addressing conflicts, focus on understanding your partner's perspective rather than defending your own.
2. **Communicate with Compassion:** Approach difficult conversations with kindness, remembering that your goal is to resolve, not to win.
3. **Forgive and Move Forward:** Be willing to forgive past hurts and work together to create a solution that strengthens your relationship.

Real Talk

- What is one conflict we resolved well, and what made that resolution effective?
- How can we apply those same principles to future disagreements?

Short Prayer

Lord, thank You for guiding us through the conflicts in our relationship. Help us to remember the lessons we've learned from our past victories, and give us the wisdom and compassion to approach future challenges with grace. May we always seek understanding, choose forgiveness, and grow closer to each other and to You. Amen.

Communication & Conflict Resolution

Pause & Reflect

How do we typically handle disagreements, and how can we better listen to each other?

Plan & Promise

What's one small change we can make to communicate with more patience and grace during conflicts?

Create & Connect

Choose a song that reflects how you want to approach conflicts with love and understanding. Write down the title and explain why you chose it.

In every disagreement, it's not about who's right, but about understanding and growing closer together.

9

FINDING OUR MISSION AS A COUPLE

> *"In the same way, let your light shine before others, that they may see your good deeds and glorify your Father in heaven."*
>
> — MATTHEW 5:16

Every couple has a unique purpose, a mission that extends beyond the walls of their home. It's about discovering how you can shine your light together, serving others, and glorifying God through your relationship. But finding that mission isn't always clear—it takes reflection, prayer, and sometimes a bit of trial and error.

I recall a conversation my spouse and I had recently. We both felt a pull on our hearts to do more, to step out of our comfort zones and serve others in a meaningful way. But the question lingered—how? We wanted to find a mission that reflected both of our passions and allowed us to work together for the greater good.

That's when I thought of a quote from *Pride and Prejudice*: *"You must allow me to tell you how ardently I admire and love you."* It reminded me that our mission didn't have to be something we pursued individually; it could be something we embark on together, driven by our love for each other and our shared desire to make a difference. Like Elizabeth and Mr. Darcy, who find strength in their union, we realized our love could be the foundation for something greater.

We began by identifying our individual passions—my spouse has a heart for mentoring young people, while I'm drawn to outreach and community service. We realized that our mission could combine these passions, creating opportunities to mentor and serve together.

Our mission as a couple isn't just about what we do; it's about who we reflect through our actions. It's about showing God's love in practical ways, whether through volunteering, mentoring, or simply being a source of encouragement to those around us.

Finding our mission has been a journey, but one thing we've learned is that God often uses the things we love to guide us toward the work He has for us. While we may not have it all figured out yet, we're committed to exploring opportunities to serve together, trusting that God will lead us where we're needed most.

Next Steps

1. **Identify Your Passions:** Reflect on what you and your spouse are individually passionate about. How can these interests combine to serve others?
2. **Start Small:** Remember, your mission doesn't have to be big to make an impact. Look for simple ways to serve together, whether it's in your church, community, or even within your family.
3. **Pray for Guidance:** Seek God's direction in discovering your mission as a couple. Be open to the opportunities He places in your path, even if they're unexpected.

Real Talk

- How can we discover our unique mission as a couple to serve others?
- What are some practical steps we can take to explore our mission and begin serving together?

Short Prayer

Lord, thank You for the unique gifts and passions You've given us as a couple. Help us to discover our mission to serve others and to let our light shine in a way that brings glory to You. Guide us as we step out in faith, trusting that You will use us to make a difference, no matter how small. Amen.

10

MAKING TIME TO SERVE TOGETHER

"Let us not become weary in doing good, for at the proper time we will reap a harvest if we do not give up."

— GALATIANS 6:9

Life is undeniably busy. Between the demands of work, family, and personal commitments, finding time to serve others can sometimes feel overwhelming. Yet, it's in those moments of shared service that the true strength of a relationship can be revealed. Serving together as a couple not only deepens your connection but also allows you to make a meaningful impact on those around you. The challenge, of course, lies in finding that time amidst the constant hustle and bustle of everyday life.

Consider your relationship as a love story, much like the one portrayed in *The Notebook*. Noah and Allie faced countless challenges, yet they always found ways to reconnect and prioritize their love for each other, no matter how overwhelming life became. In the same way, you and your spouse can discover opportunities to serve together, even when time feels scarce. The goal isn't to add more stress or obligations to your already full schedule; it's about strengthening the foundation of your relationship by sharing your time and talents in ways that bring you closer to each other and to those in need.

Service doesn't have to be elaborate or time-consuming to be meaningful. Small acts of kindness can carry significant weight. For instance, you might set aside an hour on the weekend to volunteer at a local shelter, or spend a Saturday morning participating in a community cleanup. Perhaps you could prepare a meal for a neighbor who's going through a tough time or offer to help a friend with a task they're struggling to complete. These moments, though brief, have the power to create lasting bonds—not only with those you serve but also between you and your spouse.

There's something special about working together toward a common goal, especially when that goal is to help others. The shared experience of service brings out the best in both of you, reminding you of your shared values and the love that brought you together. It shifts your focus from the demands of daily life to the bigger picture—how you, as a couple, can contribute to the well-being of others. This shared mission gives your relationship a new layer of meaning, one that transcends the ordinary and becomes a testament to the strength of your union.

Next Steps

1. **Schedule It In:** Treat service time like a priority by putting it on the calendar, just like a date night or meeting.
2. **Start Small:** Begin with manageable tasks that fit your schedule, and gradually build from there.
3. **Look for Opportunities:** Service opportunities are all around you. Stay alert for ways to serve in your community, church, or among friends.

Real Talk

- How can you make time in your busy schedule to serve others together?
- What are some small, manageable ways you can begin serving together this week?

Short Prayer

Lord, help us to make time in our busy lives to serve others together. Give us the wisdom to prioritize what truly matters and the strength to keep doing good, even when we feel weary. May our acts of service reflect Your love and bring us closer to each other and to You. Amen.

11

SUPPORTING EACH OTHER'S PASSIONS IN SERVICE

"Again, truly, I tell you that if two of you on earth agree about anything they ask for, it will be done for them by my Father in heaven. For where two or three gather in my name, there am I with them."

— MATTHEW 18:19-20

One of the most beautiful parts of marriage is how our unique passions and talents can complement each other, especially in service to others. But supporting different interests can be challenging—it requires understanding, flexibility, and a willingness to step into each other's world.

I remember when my spouse first expressed a desire to mentor at-risk youth. It was something they felt deeply about, but it wasn't a cause I had ever considered before. I found myself wondering how I could be supportive when our interests didn't fully align. Then I recalled a scene from *La La Land* where Mia tells Sebastian, *"People love what other people are passionate about."* That quote resonated with me—I realized that I didn't need to share the same passion to appreciate and support it. The key was to love how much it meant to them.

Supporting each other's passions, even when they differ, builds a stronger partnership. For us, it meant getting involved in each other's activities, even in a small role. I volunteered at the mentoring program, not because it was my passion, but because it was theirs. In return, they helped with my community outreach events.

We learned that it's not about having the same interests but sharing the journey. It's about recognizing the value in what your partner loves and standing by them, whether through active participation or encouragement. These experiences have strengthened our relationship and broadened our perspectives, allowing us to grow together in unexpected ways.

As we continued to support each other, we realized that it wasn't just about the activities themselves but about the deeper connection we were building. Stepping into each others world says, *"I see you, and I'm here with you."* This engagement has transformed our relationship, and over time, these shared experiences have become cherished memories. True partnership is about embracing and celebrating each other's passions, no matter how different they are.

Next Steps

1. **Communicate Openly:** Talk about your passions and how you'd like to be supported. Understand that support can take many forms, from active participation to simply offering encouragement.
2. **Be Flexible:** Be open to stepping out of your comfort zone to support your spouse's passions, even if it's not something you would naturally gravitate toward.
3. **Celebrate Each Other's Wins:** Acknowledge and celebrate the positive impact your partner makes, reinforcing their passion and showing appreciation.

Real Talk

- How can we support each other's passions and talents in serving others?
- What are some specific ways we can get involved in or encourage each other's service activities?

Short Prayer

Lord, thank You for the unique passions and talents You've placed within us. Help us support each other by using these gifts to serve others. Teach us to appreciate and encourage one another's contributions, knowing that together, we can make a greater impact on Your kingdom. Amen.

12

SERVING IN SMALL WAYS EVERY DAY

"Your word is a lamp for my feet, a light on my path."

— PSALM 119:105

Serving others doesn't always require grand gestures or elaborate plans. In fact, it's often the small, everyday acts of kindness that have the most profound impact. These simple acts not only bless those around us but also strengthen the bond between couples as they grow together in their shared purpose.

Consider the story of Michael and Rachel. Married for five years, they both lead busy lives with demanding careers. Yet, they've made it a priority to find small ways to serve others daily. Whether it's making an extra lunch to give to someone in need, helping a neighbor with groceries, or sending an encouraging text to a friend, these small acts of kindness have become a cornerstone of their relationship. Through these gestures, they've discovered that serving others doesn't just brighten someone else's day—it also brings them closer as a couple.

This reminds me of that famous moment in *Jerry Maguire* when Jerry says, *"You complete me."* While the line is about love, it also speaks to the way couples can complete each other through shared purpose and small, loving actions. Serving together, even in the simplest ways, allows couples to fill in the gaps for one another, fostering a sense of completeness and unity that strengthens their bond.

As couples walk through life together, they can find small, meaningful ways to serve others that align with their shared values and goals. These daily acts of service, though seemingly small, accumulate over time, creating a life rich with purpose and connection.

Michael and Rachel's story is a powerful reminder of the impact that small, consistent acts of kindness can have. By serving together in these everyday ways, they've found a deeper sense of unity and fulfillment in their relationship. They've also experienced the joy of seeing how their small efforts can make a significant difference in the lives of others. These acts, guided by love and intention, demonstrate that even the simplest gestures can bring light to others and deepen the bond between a couple.

Next Steps

1. **Be Intentional:** Look for opportunities to serve others in your daily routine. Whether it's offering a smile, a helping hand, or a word of encouragement, these small acts can make a big difference.
2. **Serve Together:** Find ways to serve as a team. Even small acts, like making dinner for a friend in need or praying for someone together, can strengthen your bond.
3. **Reflect on God's Guidance:** Let God's Word guide your actions. As you seek to serve others, ask for His direction in finding the opportunities that align with His purpose for you as a couple.

Real Talk

- What small acts of service can we do each day to bless others and grow closer as a couple?
- How can we be more intentional about noticing the needs around us and responding with kindness?

Short Prayer

Lord, help us to see the opportunities to serve others in our everyday lives. Guide us to act with kindness and compassion, even in the smallest of ways. As we serve together, may we grow closer to each other and to You, shining Your light in the world around us. Amen.

Serving Others Together

Pause & Reflect

How can we serve others as a couple and make a difference together?

Plan & Promise

What's one small step we can take this week to begin serving others together?

Create & Connect

Make a list of three small acts of service you can do together this week.

Our love for each other shines brightest when we serve others together, hand in hand.

13

NURTURING EMOTIONAL INTIMACY

"Above all, love each other deeply, because love covers over a multitude of sins."

— 1 PETER 4:8

In the midst of daily responsibilities—work, household chores, parenting, and endless tasks—emotional closeness can sometimes get lost in the shuffle. However, cultivating this deep connection is crucial for a thriving relationship. It's not just about finding time but about making time to connect on a level where both partners feel understood, valued, and truly loved.

The lyrics from the song *I Will Follow You into the Dark* by Death Cab for Cutie resonate deeply: *"If there's no one beside you when your soul embarks, then I'll follow you into the dark."* This line beautifully captures the essence of emotional intimacy—being there for each other, no matter what, and prioritizing the bond that ties you together. True connection isn't about grand gestures; it's about the quiet moments of understanding and support that build trust and deepen your relationship.

When you focus on fostering emotional closeness, you create a space where love can thrive, even in the midst of life's challenges. It's about choosing to invest in your relationship—listening more intently, being more present, and showing love in the small, everyday moments. These simple actions are the foundation of a strong emotional bond.

Start by setting aside time each day to check in with each other—share your thoughts, feelings, and experiences without distractions. Whether it's a few minutes in the morning over coffee or a quiet conversation before bed, these moments of connection can make all the difference. Additionally, practicing gratitude is another powerful way to deepen your connection. Expressing appreciation for the small things your partner does, which often go unnoticed, can strengthen your bond and create a deeper sense of unity.

As you navigate the demands of daily life, remember that making time for emotional connection isn't just about finding moments but about creating them. It's about making your relationship a priority, knowing that these small investments will pay off in a deeper, more meaningful connection that can withstand any challenge life throws your way.

Next Steps

1. **Daily Check-Ins:** Ask how your partner is feeling and listen. A few minutes of genuine conversation can strengthen your connection.
2. **Show Gratitude:** Regularly appreciate the small things your partner does. Gratitude fosters closeness and love.
3. **Be Present:** Put away distractions during your time together. Whether it's during meals, while talking, or even watching TV, being fully present is key to deepening your bond.

Real Talk

- What are some ways you can prioritize emotional connection amid your daily responsibilities?
- How can you make more time for meaningful conversations and deepen your relationship?

Short Prayer

Lord, help us to prioritize our emotional connection in this relationship. Teach us to love each other deeply, to listen with our hearts, and to create a space where our bond can grow stronger each day. Guide us in strengthening the relationship You have blessed us with, so that we may reflect Your love in our lives together. Amen.

14

DAILY ACTS OF APPRECIATION

"Give thanks in all circumstances; for this is God's will for you in Christ Jesus."

— 1 THESSALONIANS 5:18

It's easy to get swept up in the busyness of life, and when that happens, we can sometimes overlook the little things our partner does each day. Yet, expressing gratitude, even in the smallest ways, can have a profound impact on our relationship. It's not just about acknowledging the big gestures; it's about noticing and appreciating the everyday acts that often go unnoticed.

I recall a time when my spouse and I were navigating a particularly hectic season. With work, family commitments, and an endless to-do list, we both felt the strain. Amidst all the chaos, I started to feel a sense of disconnection. It wasn't that our love had faded—it was simply that we were so consumed by our responsibilities that we forgot to pause and recognize the ways we were supporting each other daily.

The turning point came when we made a conscious effort to express appreciation for even the smallest acts of kindness. Whether it was acknowledging the effort put into making dinner, taking out the trash, or simply offering a warm smile, these small expressions of gratitude became our way of reconnecting and reminding each other that we are seen and valued.

Incorporating daily acts of appreciation fosters a spirit of gratitude that uplifts both partners and strengthens the relationship. Expressing thanks doesn't need to be elaborate. It can be as simple as leaving a note of encouragement, sending a thoughtful text during the day, or verbally recognizing something your partner did that made a difference.

Over time, these small acts of appreciation build a solid foundation of love and respect, helping the relationship thrive even in the busiest seasons of life. They serve as a daily reminder that we see each other, value each other, and are grateful for one another's presence, no matter how hectic life becomes.

Next Steps

1. **Verbal Acknowledgment:** Make it a point to verbally appreciate something your partner does each day, no matter how small.
2. **Leave Notes:** Write short notes of appreciation and leave them where your partner will find them—on the bathroom mirror, in their lunch, or on the dashboard of their car.
3. **Thoughtful Gestures:** Perform small acts of kindness, like preparing their favorite snack or doing a chore they dislike, as a way of showing appreciation.

Real Talk

- How can we express appreciation for each other daily, even in small ways?
- What are some specific actions or words that make you feel most appreciated?

Short Prayer

Lord, help us to cultivate a heart of gratitude in our relationship. Teach us to see and appreciate the small and big ways we support each other daily. May our expressions of thanks bring us closer together and reflect Your love in our lives. Amen.

15

UNDERSTANDING PHYSICAL INTIMACY

"The husband should fulfill his marital duty to his wife, and likewise the wife to her husband."

— 1 CORINTHIANS 7:3

Physical intimacy is an important part of any marriage, serving as a beautiful way for couples to express love, affection, and connection. It's more than just a physical act; it's about emotional closeness and mutual care that strengthens the bond between husband and wife. Like any aspect of a relationship, it takes a bit of effort and intention to keep this connection strong and healthy.

For some couples, physical intimacy feels natural, while for others, it might take a little more time and understanding to embrace its importance fully. The key is recognizing that it's not just about meeting physical needs—it's about building trust, creating emotional security, and deepening the love you share. In marriage, physical intimacy is a special way to show love and commitment, making both partners feel valued, desired, and connected.

When nurtured with love, respect, and care, physical intimacy becomes a source of joy and closeness that benefits the overall health of your relationship. It's important to remember that this connection is about more than just the physical aspect—it also includes being there for each other emotionally and spiritually.

One way to nurture physical intimacy is by creating a safe, open space where both of you feel comfortable sharing your needs and desires. This includes being in tune with each other's feelings, showing patience, and finding ways to express affection outside of the bedroom too. Simple gestures like holding hands, hugging, or spending quality time together help keep that sense of closeness alive.

It's also helpful to make time for physical intimacy, even when life gets busy. Whether it's planning regular date nights, finding little moments to reconnect during the day, or just being intentional about showing affection, these small efforts can make a big difference.

By focusing on physical intimacy with love and care, you can strengthen your connection, deepen your bond, and enjoy a richer, more fulfilling relationship together.

Next Steps

1. **Communicate Openly:** Share your needs, desires, and boundaries. Open communication builds trust and mutual understanding.
2. **Prioritize Quality Time:** Make time for each other regularly, whether through date nights, quiet evenings at home, or spontaneous moments of affection. This helps maintain the connection that feeds physical intimacy.
3. **Express Affection Daily:** Small acts of physical touch, like holding hands or giving a hug, can reinforce your bond and keep the connection strong.

Real Talk

- What does physical intimacy mean to you as a couple, and how can you nurture it more intentionally?
- How can you create a safe space to discuss your needs and desires related to physical intimacy?

Short Prayer

Lord, thank You for the gift of physical intimacy in marriage. Help us to nurture this aspect of our relationship with love, care, and understanding. Guide us as we seek to deepen our connection, and may our physical intimacy be a reflection of the love and commitment we share. Amen.

16

BALANCING HEART & BODY

"My beloved is mine and I am his; he browses among the lilies."

— SONG OF SOLOMON 2:16

In a healthy relationship, both physical and emotional closeness are key to building a strong, lasting connection. Physical intimacy shows love through touch, while emotional intimacy deepens trust, understanding, and emotional security. The challenge for many couples is finding a balance that nurtures both, helping the relationship grow.

Think of the song *I'm Yours* by Jason Mraz, where he sings, *"Open up your plans and, damn, you're free. Look into your heart and you'll find love, love, love."* These lyrics capture the idea of balancing heart and body in a relationship. It's about being open, vulnerable, and embracing both the emotional and physical sides of love. When you achieve this balance, you create a harmony that strengthens your bond.

Balancing physical and emotional intimacy is important because one supports the other. Emotional closeness builds the trust you need, while physical intimacy reinforces that connection, allowing you to express love in a meaningful way.

To keep this balance, be intentional about both aspects of your relationship. Spend time having meaningful conversations, sharing your thoughts, dreams, and feelings. These moments of emotional connection make physical closeness more meaningful. At the same time, don't forget the power of physical touch—whether it's a hug, a kiss, or holding hands. These small gestures help maintain the physical connection that complements your emotional bond.

Another key to balance is understanding and respecting each other's needs. Talk openly about what makes you feel loved and connected, both emotionally and physically. This creates a safe space where both partners feel valued and cherished.

Next Steps

1. **Prioritize Communication:** Regularly check in with each other about how you're feeling emotionally and physically. Open, honest communication is key to maintaining balance.
2. **Make Time for Both:** Set aside time for activities that nurture both your emotional and physical connection, whether it's a deep conversation over dinner or a spontaneous date night.
3. **Respect Each Other's Needs:** Understand that each of you may have different needs when it comes to emotional and physical intimacy. Be willing to listen and adapt to ensure both aspects are nurtured.

Real Talk

- How can you balance physical and emotional intimacy to ensure both are nurtured?
- What are some specific ways you can intentionally nurture both your emotional and physical connection?

Short Prayer

Lord, help us to balance the heart and body in our relationship, nurturing both emotional and physical intimacy. Teach us to communicate openly, to love deeply, and to honor each other's needs. May our love for one another reflect the beauty and passion You have designed for marriage. Amen.

Emotional & Physical Intimacy

Pause & Reflect

How can we nurture our emotional and physical intimacy in a way that strengthens our bond?

Plan & Promise

What's one small action we can take this week to foster both emotional and physical closeness?

Create & Connect

Write a short note of appreciation to each other, focusing on something specific about your emotional and physical connection that you cherish.

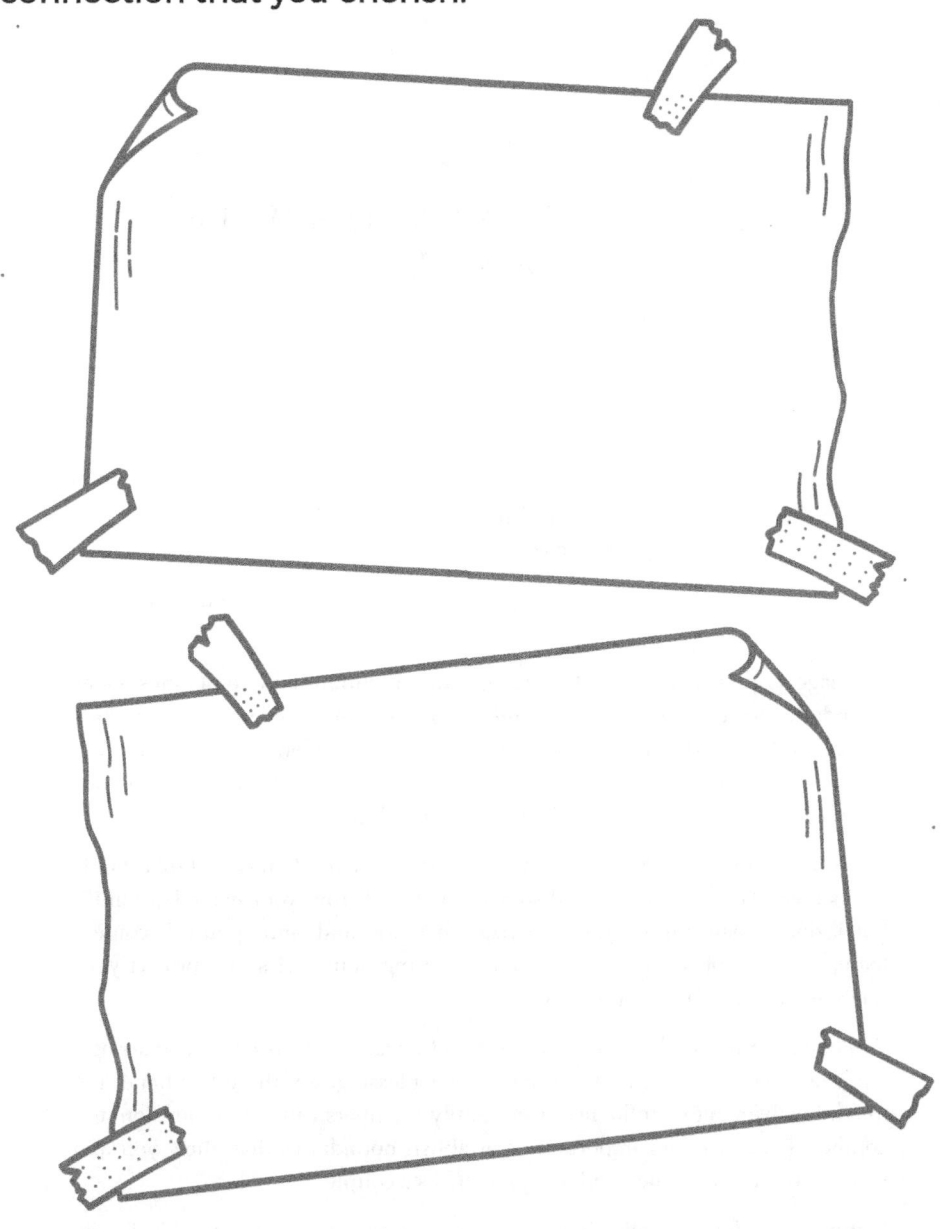

True intimacy is not just in touch, but in being fully present for each other, heart and soul.

17

SETTING BOUNDARIES WITH FAMILY

"That is why a man leaves his father and mother and is united to his wife, and they become one flesh."

— GENESIS 2:24

Marriage is a special bond that needs care, attention, and sometimes, clear boundaries to keep it strong. While relationships with extended family can be a source of love and support, they can also bring challenges if not carefully managed. Balancing the involvement of extended family with the needs of your marriage is key to maintaining a healthy relationship.

When you get married, you and your spouse create a new family unit that stands on its own. This doesn't mean distancing yourself from your extended family, but it does mean putting your marriage first. You and your spouse become a team, and part of being a strong team is setting boundaries that protect your relationship from outside pressures.

Extended family can have both positive and negative effects on your marriage. On one hand, their support can be a great blessing. On the other hand, too much involvement or influence from family members can lead to tension and conflict. That's why it's important to establish boundaries that allow you and your spouse to stay united and independent as a couple.

Setting boundaries might include having open conversations with family members about their role in your lives. It could mean agreeing on how much time you spend with extended family, how involved they are in your decisions, and how you handle conflicts that arise. Boundaries can also involve deciding what personal information you share with family members to ensure your privacy is respected.

The key to setting effective boundaries is being united in your approach. Both you and your spouse need to agree on what boundaries are necessary and why. This unity helps you stand firm together and protect your relationship from outside influences that could cause strain.

Next Steps

1. **Communicate as a Team:** Discuss and agree on the boundaries you need to set with extended family. Present a united front when communicating these boundaries to family members.
2. **Prioritize Your Marriage:** Ensure that your marriage comes first in all situations. Make decisions that support the health and unity of your relationship, even if it means making difficult choices about family involvement.
3. **Be Respectful but Firm:** Setting boundaries doesn't mean shutting out family; it means creating healthy limits that protect your marriage. Communicate these boundaries with love, respect, and clarity.

Real Talk

- How do our relationships with extended family impact our marriage, and what boundaries can we set to protect our relationship?
- How can we support each other in maintaining these boundaries while still honoring our relationships with extended family?

Short Prayer

Lord, thank You for the gift of family and the support they provide. Help us to honor our relationships with extended family while prioritizing our marriage above all else. Guide us as we set boundaries that protect our unity and love. May we always seek to glorify You in the way we relate to each other and to those around us. Amen.

18

HONORING PARENTS, PRIORITIZING MARRIAGE

"Honor your father and your mother, so that you may live long in the land the Lord your God is giving you."

— EXODUS 20:12

Balancing the need to honor your parents with the equally important call to prioritize your marriage can sometimes feel like a difficult juggling act. Both relationships are essential, but when they conflict, it's important to find a way to respect your parents while keeping your marriage strong and united.

I remember a time when my spouse and I faced this challenge directly. We were both raised to deeply respect our parents, and we genuinely wanted to honor them. However, there were moments when our parents' expectations or opinions didn't align with what was best for our marriage. We realized that we needed to handle these situations carefully to avoid tension and protect our relationship.

This situation reminded me of the movie *The Notebook*. Noah and Allie come from different backgrounds, and their love is tested by family expectations and social pressures. Despite these challenges, they ultimately choose each other, prioritizing their relationship even when it means going against their parents' wishes. Like them, we recognized that while it's important to honor our parents, our marriage had to come first.

Honoring our parents doesn't mean always agreeing with them or letting their influence overshadow our marriage. Instead, it means treating them with respect, valuing their wisdom, and finding ways to honor them that don't compromise our relationship.

To balance these responsibilities, my spouse and I agreed to discuss our parents' needs and opinions together, making sure we were on the same page before making any decisions. We also set boundaries that allowed us to honor our parents while still prioritizing our marriage. This approach helped us maintain harmony in our family while keeping our relationship strong.

Next Steps

1. **Communicate Openly:** Discuss with your spouse how to honor your parents while prioritizing your marriage. Ensure you are united in your approach and present a consistent message to your families.
2. **Set Healthy Boundaries:** Establish boundaries that allow you to show respect to your parents without compromising your marriage. Boundaries can include deciding together how much influence your parents have on your decisions.
3. **Seek Balance:** Honor your parents by valuing their advice and showing respect, but make sure your marriage remains your top priority. Remember, your spouse is your partner in life, and your unity is essential.

Real Talk

- How can you balance honoring your parents while prioritizing your marriage?
- What boundaries can you set to ensure that your marriage remains your primary focus?

Short Prayer

Lord, thank You for the gift of marriage and the blessing of family. Help us to honor our parents with love and respect while keeping our marriage strong and united. Give us wisdom to navigate these relationships in a way that glorifies You and strengthens our bond as husband and wife. Amen.

19

CREATING FAMILY TRADITIONS

"But as for me and my household, we will serve the Lord."

— JOSHUA 24:15

Family traditions are the threads that weave a family together, creating a sense of belonging, continuity, and shared purpose. For couples, building or continuing meaningful traditions is a wonderful way to strengthen their bond and create lasting memories. Whether you're carrying forward traditions from your own childhood or creating new ones together, these practices help shape your family's identity and values.

Think of the song *We Are Family* by Sister Sledge, where the lyrics celebrate the strength and unity that come from being a family. Just as the song suggests, traditions bring family members closer, fostering a sense of togetherness and shared identity. When couples make an effort to establish or maintain traditions, they're building a legacy that reflects their love, values, and shared goals.

Creating family traditions is about making intentional choices that reflect the life you want to build together. These traditions can take many forms—weekly family dinners, holiday celebrations, bedtime prayers, or Sunday afternoon walks. Whatever they are, these rituals become the building blocks of your family's story.

For couples just starting out, it's important to talk about which traditions from your own childhood you'd like to bring into your marriage and what new ones you'd like to create together. Maybe it's a commitment to volunteering as a family, establishing a unique holiday tradition, or setting aside time each week to connect and reflect. The key is to choose traditions that resonate with both of you and reflect the values you want to instill in your family.

By intentionally creating and maintaining these traditions, you're not only building a strong foundation for your relationship but also creating lasting memories that will be cherished for years to come.

Next Steps

1. **Reflect on the Past:** Discuss the traditions you each grew up with. Which ones were meaningful to you, and which would you like to carry forward into your own family?
2. **Create New Traditions:** Think about the values and experiences you want to prioritize in your family. What new traditions can you create that reflect these?
3. **Be Intentional:** Make a plan to incorporate these traditions into your life regularly, ensuring they become a meaningful part of your family's rhythm and identity.

Real Talk

- What family traditions or practices do you want to carry forward or create together?
- How can these traditions help shape the values and identity of your family?

Short Prayer

Lord, thank You for the gift of family and the traditions that help us grow closer to You and to each other. Guide us as we create and carry forward practices that reflect our faith and values. May these traditions bring joy, unity, and a lasting legacy of love in our home. Amen.

20

DEALING WITH FAMILY STRESS

> *"If it is possible, as far as it depends on you, live at peace with everyone."*
>
> — ROMANS 12:18

Family is a source of love and support, but it can also bring stress, especially when expectations and obligations become overwhelming. Whether it's dealing with differing opinions, handling conflicts, or managing the pressures that come with family responsibilities, it's important to approach these situations with care and wisdom. The goal is to manage stress in a way that protects your relationship and maintains peace.

I remember a time when my spouse and I faced conflicting family expectations during the holidays. Both of our families had different traditions and demands, and we felt torn in multiple directions. The pressure quickly started to affect our relationship. We realized that if we didn't take control, the stress would ruin the joy and peace we wanted to experience during that season.

What helped us was learning that while we couldn't control everything, we could control how we responded. Instead of letting stress take over, we chose to communicate openly with each other and our families. We set clear boundaries and made decisions together, keeping our relationship as the top priority.

Managing family stress often involves having tough conversations, setting boundaries, and being honest about what you can and can't do. It's about finding a balance that respects your family commitments without sacrificing your peace or the health of your relationship. By approaching these situations with patience and understanding, you can handle family stress in a way that encourages harmony rather than conflict.

Next Steps

1. **Communicate as a Team:** Discuss family expectations together and decide how to handle them as a united front. Make sure you're both comfortable with the decisions you make.
2. **Set Boundaries:** Establish clear boundaries with your families to protect your time, energy, and relationship. This might include setting limits on visits, agreeing on how to handle conflicts, or deciding how much involvement family members have in certain aspects of your life.
3. **Practice Patience and Grace:** Family stress is often unavoidable, but how you handle it makes all the difference. Approach conflicts with patience, grace, and a willingness to find peaceful solutions.

Real Talk

- How can we manage stress or conflict that arises from family expectations or obligations?
- What boundaries can we set to protect our relationship while still honoring our families?

Short Prayer

Lord, thank You for the gift of family and the love that comes with it. Help us to manage the stress and conflicts that sometimes arise with wisdom and grace. Guide us as we seek to live at peace with everyone while protecting our relationship. May our actions reflect Your love and bring harmony into our lives. Amen.

Family Dynamics & Boundaries

Pause & Reflect

How can we set healthy boundaries with our families while keeping our marriage strong?

Plan & Promise

What's one small step we can take this week to ensure our marriage remains the priority when navigating family dynamics?

Create & Connect

Create a plan for how you'll balance time between extended family and each other.

A strong marriage is built on love, trust, and boundaries that protect the heart of the relationship.

21

FAITH AND FINANCES

"For where your treasure is, there your heart will be also."

— MATTHEW 6:21

Money plays a big role in any marriage, influencing everything from daily decisions to long-term goals. For couples who share a faith, financial decisions aren't just about managing resources—they're also about aligning their spending and saving habits with their beliefs. How a couple views and handles money can have a significant impact on their relationship, and bringing faith into financial decisions can help create unity, peace, and purpose.

Talking about money can sometimes lead to tension, especially if it's not handled with care and understanding. Different backgrounds, experiences, and attitudes toward money often result in differing perspectives. One partner might be more focused on saving and planning for the future, while the other might prioritize enjoying the present. These differences are natural but require open conversations and mutual respect to find a balanced approach.

For couples, managing money in a way that reflects their shared values can strengthen their relationship. When faith is at the center of financial decisions, the focus shifts from simply accumulating wealth to using resources wisely, giving generously, and making choices that reflect their beliefs.

Couples can start by having honest discussions about their financial goals, priorities, and concerns. Talking about how they want to use their resources to serve their values can help create a sense of purpose and unity in their financial decisions. Whether it's budgeting, saving, investing, or giving, approaching finances with a shared perspective ensures that both partners feel valued and supported.

Trust is also a key factor—trust in each other and in the belief that their needs will be met. Financial challenges are a part of life, but when couples trust each other and work together with a shared purpose, they can face those challenges with confidence and peace.

Next Steps

1. **Align Your Values:** Discuss your financial goals and how your faith influences them. Ensure that your financial decisions reflect your shared values and priorities.
2. **Practice Stewardship:** View your resources as gifts from God, to be managed wisely and used for His glory. This includes budgeting, saving, giving, and spending in a way that honors Him.
3. **Communicate Regularly:** Make it a habit to check in with each other about finances. Regular communication helps prevent misunderstandings and keeps you both on the same page.

Real Talk

- How do we view money, and what role does our faith play in our financial decisions?
- What steps can we take to ensure our financial practices align with our values and faith?

Short Prayer

Lord, thank You for the resources You have entrusted to us. Help us to use them wisely and in a way that honors You. Guide us as we make financial decisions, and may our choices reflect our faith and bring us closer to You and to each other. Amen.

22

SETTING FINANCIAL GOALS TOGETHER

"The plans of the diligent lead to profit as surely as haste leads to poverty."

— PROVERBS 21:5

Setting financial goals together is a key part of building a strong and unified marriage. When those goals align with your values, they become more than just financial targets—they reflect your shared priorities, beliefs, and commitment to each other. However, working together to define and achieve these goals takes clear communication, mutual respect, and a shared vision for the future.

I remember when my spouse and I first sat down to discuss our financial goals. The conversation felt a bit overwhelming at first, as we had different ideas about what we wanted to achieve and how to get there. But as we talked, we realized that we both wanted the same thing: a future where our finances reflected our values and allowed us to live out what's important to us.

This reminds me of the song *Grow Old with You* by Adam Sandler, where the lyrics talk about all the small, everyday ways a couple supports each other as they build a life together. Just like in the song, setting financial goals isn't just about the destination—it's about the journey, adjusting and adapting along the way, while staying focused on what truly matters.

When you set financial goals with intention and patience, you're more likely to achieve them. For us, this meant creating a budget that reflected our values, prioritizing things like saving, giving, and living within our means. We also committed to regularly reviewing our goals and adjusting them as needed, knowing that flexibility is key to staying on track.

One of the best parts of setting financial goals together is seeing how they support both our relationship and our future. Whether it's saving for a home, paying off debt, or setting aside money for causes we care about, each goal brings us closer to a future that reflects our shared values and strengthens our bond.

Next Steps

1. **Align Your Goals:** Start by discussing your spiritual values and how they can guide your financial goals. Make sure your goals reflect your commitment to stewardship, generosity, and living with purpose.
2. **Create a Plan:** Develop a plan that includes a budget, savings strategy, and timelines for achieving your goals. Regularly review your progress and make adjustments as needed.
3. **Stay Flexible:** Life is full of unexpected changes. Be willing to adapt your goals and plans while keeping your shared vision in mind.

Real Talk

- What financial goals can we set together that align with our spiritual values?
- How can we ensure that our financial decisions support our long-term vision for our marriage and our faith?

Short Prayer

Lord, thank You for the resources You have provided us. Help us to set financial goals that honor You and align with our spiritual values. Guide us as we plan for our future, and give us the wisdom to make decisions that reflect our faith and commitment to each other. Amen.

23

MAKING DECISIONS AS A TEAM

"She considers a field and buys it; out of her earnings she plants a vineyard."

— PROVERBS 31:16

Financial decisions are a big part of any marriage, and it's important that both partners are actively involved in making these choices. When both of you participate in financial decisions, it not only strengthens your relationship but also ensures that your financial goals align with your shared values and priorities. A unified approach helps avoid misunderstandings, builds trust, and leads to better outcomes for your family.

In many marriages, one partner might naturally take the lead in handling finances, like managing the budget, paying bills, or making investment choices. While it's natural to have different strengths, it's crucial that both partners have a say in major financial decisions. This doesn't mean you have to agree on every detail, but it does mean approaching decisions together with respect and a shared sense of purpose.

Making thoughtful financial decisions as a team is important for a strong marriage. Whether you're buying a home, planning for retirement, or managing debt, involving both partners in these discussions ensures that your financial goals reflect your values and that you're both committed to the decisions you make together.

To work as a team, set aside regular times to talk about your finances. These conversations should be open and honest, allowing each of you to share your thoughts, concerns, and goals. It's also helpful to establish a process for making decisions together—whether that's agreeing to consult each other on purchases over a certain amount or collaborating on a long-term financial plan. By approaching finances as partners, you build trust and ensure that both of you are invested in your financial future.

Next Steps

1. **Communicate Regularly:** Schedule regular financial check-ins to discuss your goals, budgets, and any upcoming financial decisions. This keeps both partners informed and involved.
2. **Respect Each Other's Input:** Recognize that both of you bring valuable perspectives to financial decisions. Listen to each other's ideas and concerns, and work together to find solutions that satisfy both of you.
3. **Establish a Decision-Making Process:** Agree on how you'll handle major financial decisions, whether it's setting spending limits that require mutual consent or deciding on a process for setting and achieving long-term goals.

Real Talk

- How can we ensure we're both involved in major financial decisions?
- What steps can we take to improve our communication and collaboration on financial matters?

Short Prayer

Lord, thank You for the wisdom and resources You have provided us. Help us to make financial decisions together with unity, respect, and a shared commitment to honoring You. Guide us as we seek to be good stewards of what You have given us, and may our decisions reflect our love for each other and our trust in You. Amen.

24

PRAYING OVER OUR FINANCES

"If any of you lacks wisdom, you should ask God, who gives generously to all without finding fault, and it will be given to you."

—JAMES 1:5

In marriage, financial decisions are often some of the most significant and challenging choices we make together. From budgeting and saving to investing and giving, how we handle our finances shows what's important to us. For us, making these decisions with care and in line with our beliefs has been essential to maintaining unity and peace in our marriage.

I remember when we faced a tough financial decision. We were unsure of the best path forward, and the weight of the choice was heavy on both of us. It became clear that we needed more than just practical advice—we needed guidance beyond ourselves. That's when we decided to turn to prayer, seeking clarity and wisdom before making any final decisions.

Involving prayer in our financial decisions has brought us closer and helped us find peace in our choices. By praying together and seeking guidance, we've found that our decisions are not only wiser but also more aligned with what's best for us as a couple. Prayer has become the foundation of our financial planning, helping us approach each decision with a sense of purpose.

We make it a habit to bring our financial concerns and questions into our prayers regularly. Whether it's deciding on a major purchase, considering an investment, or planning our giving, we take time to pray about it together. This practice helps us stay focused on what truly matters and make decisions that reflect our values and strengthen our relationship.

Next Steps

1. **Pray Before Deciding:** Make it a habit to pray together before making any major financial decisions. Ask God for wisdom, clarity, and peace as you consider your options.
2. **Seek Biblical Guidance:** As you pray, consult scripture to see what God's Word says about the financial decisions you're facing. Let biblical principles guide your choices and actions.
3. **Trust in God's Provision:** Remember that God is the ultimate provider. Approach your finances with faith, trusting that He will guide you to make decisions that honor Him and benefit your family.

Real Talk

- How can we make financial decisions prayerfully and in consultation with biblical principles?
- What steps can we take to ensure that our financial planning is rooted in our faith and aligned with God's will?

Short Prayer

Lord, we thank You for the blessings and resources You have entrusted to us. As we make financial decisions, guide us with Your wisdom and help us to align our choices with Your will. May our finances reflect our faith, and may we trust in Your provision as we seek to honor You in all we do. Amen.

Financial Stewardship & Decision-Making

Pause & Reflect

How can we better align our financial decisions with our faith and shared values?

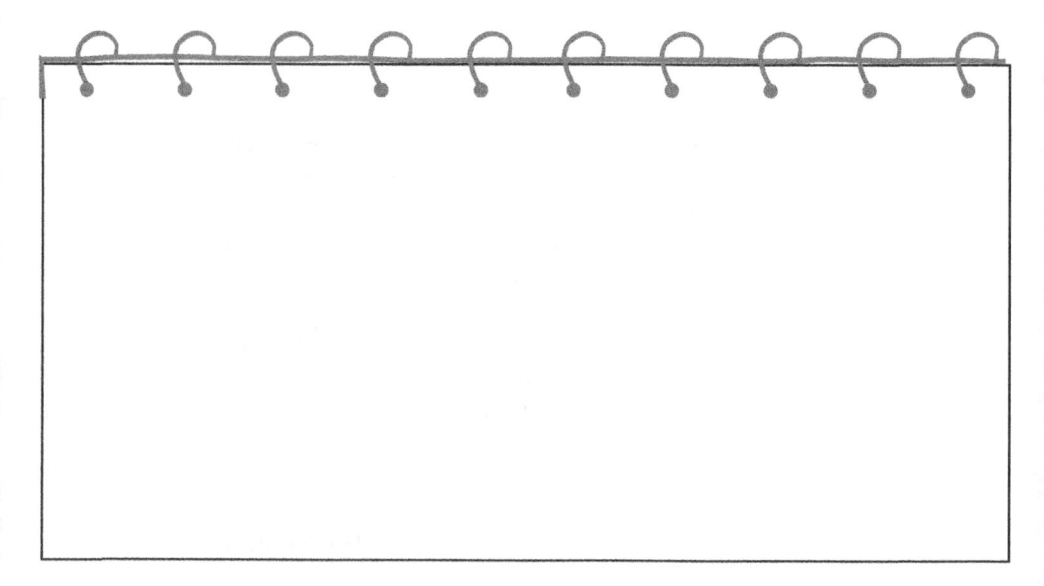

Plan & Promise

What's one step we can take this week to improve our financial stewardship and work toward our shared financial goals?

Create & Connect

Create a simple budget that reflects your shared values. Prioritize categories like giving, saving, and spending on what matters most to both of you.

When we manage our resources together with faith and purpose, we build a future that reflects our love for each other and our trust in God.

25

INTENTIONAL CO-PARENTING

> *"These commandments that I give you today are to be on your hearts. Impress them on your children. Talk about them when you sit at home and when you walk along the road, when you lie down and when you get up."*
>
> — DEUTERONOMY 6:6-7

Co-parenting in a faith-centered home requires intentional effort, mutual respect, and a shared vision for how you want to raise your children. It's about working together as a team to create an environment where your children not only learn about faith but also see it lived out daily in your actions, decisions, and interactions. Being intentional about co-parenting means you prioritize your child's spiritual development as much as their physical, emotional, and intellectual growth.

This passage from Deuteronomy emphasizes the importance of consistently teaching and modeling God's commandments to your children. It encourages parents to make faith an integral part of everyday life, weaving it into conversations, activities, and routines. As co-parents, your goal is to ensure that your children are grounded in their faith and equipped to carry those values into adulthood.

To be more intentional about co-parenting in a faith-centered home, start by establishing clear and shared goals for your family's spiritual life. Discuss how you want to incorporate faith into your daily routines, such as through family prayers, Bible readings, attending church, or serving together in your community. Consistency is key; the more your children see you both actively engaging in and prioritizing faith, the more it will become a natural and essential part of their lives.

Another important aspect of intentional co-parenting is maintaining open and respectful communication with each other, especially when it comes to decisions about your children's spiritual education. Be united in your approach, ensuring that both parents are aligned in their expectations and practices. This unity provides stability for your children and reinforces the values you wish to instill in them.

Next Steps

1. **Create a Faith-Centered Routine:** Incorporate daily practices like prayers or devotionals to show the importance of faith in everyday life.
2. **Be a United Front:** Communicate with your co-parent to align on parenting approaches, reinforcing shared values for your children.
3. **Lead by Example:** Model the faith-centered behavior you want your children to adopt. Let them see you praying, reading the Bible, and serving others, so they learn the importance of these practices through your example.

Real Talk

1. How can we be more intentional about co-parenting and raising our children in a faith-centered home?
2. What specific practices or routines can we implement to ensure our children grow up with a strong spiritual foundation?

Short Prayer

Lord, thank You for the gift of children and the privilege of raising them in a faith-centered home. Help us to be intentional in our co-parenting, working together to guide our children in Your ways. Give us wisdom and unity as we seek to model and teach Your love and truth. Amen.

26

MODELING VALUES FOR OUR KIDS

"Start children off on the way they should go, and even when they are old they will not turn from it."

— PROVERBS 22:6

As parents, we all want our kids to grow up with strong values that guide them through life. Whether it's kindness, honesty, responsibility, or faith, these values shape who they become. But teaching values isn't just about having serious conversations—it's about showing them through our everyday actions. Our kids are always watching, and what they see often speaks louder than what we say.

It's not enough to just tell our kids what's right—we need to set an example by living out those values ourselves. If we want them to grow up being kind, we need to show kindness in our daily interactions. If honesty is important, they need to see us being truthful, even when it's tough. The way we live every day becomes the guide our kids use to make their own choices.

For example, if you want your child to value gratitude, start by showing appreciation for the small things. Thank them when they help out, express gratitude to your partner in front of them, or talk about what you're grateful for at dinner. If you want them to understand respect, model that in how you treat others—whether it's how you speak to a server at a restaurant or how you talk about your coworkers at home. These small, consistent actions are what stick with them as they grow.

Consistency is key. Kids are incredibly observant, and they notice when our actions don't match our words. If we tell them to be patient but lose our temper easily, they'll see the contradiction. If we say they should be generous but hesitate to give to those in need, they'll notice that too. By living out the values we want them to embrace, we help them learn those lessons in a way that words alone never could.

Next Steps

1. **Know What Matters:** Sit down together and identify the core values that are most important to your family. Make sure these values are reflected in your daily life.
2. **Be the Example:** Show your kids what these values look like in action. Whether it's through how you handle challenges, interact with others, or make decisions, let your life be the lesson.
3. **Teach Through Everyday Moments:** Use the small, everyday moments as opportunities to teach and reinforce values. Talk about why you made certain choices, and explain how they align with your family's beliefs.

Real Talk

- What values do we want to pass on to our children, and how can we model them in our daily lives?
- How can we create more opportunities to live out these values together as a family?

Short Prayer

Lord, thank You for the precious gift of our children. Help us to live out the values we want to instill in them with integrity and consistency. Give us wisdom and strength as we guide them on the path You have set before them, and may our lives be a reflection of Your love and truth. Amen.

ENCOURAGE OTHERS BY SHARING YOUR EXPERIENCE

"Therefore encourage one another and build each other up, just as in fact you are doing."

— 1 THESSALONIANS 5:11

As a couple seeking to grow in faith and unity, your journey through this devotional has been a meaningful part of your shared walk with God. Whether it has helped you find new ways to connect spiritually, encouraged deeper conversations, or inspired you to make positive changes in your relationship, we are truly grateful that you've been on this path with us.

Would you consider helping another couple, just like you once were— seeking connection, guidance, and encouragement?

They're out there—couples who, like you, long to deepen their bond with each other and with God. And your experience could be the very encouragement they need. By sharing how this devotional has touched your life, you may inspire another couple to take that first step toward strengthening their relationship.

Here's how you can make an impact:

Your review could help...

- ...a couple find strength and joy amidst the busyness of life.
- ...partners rekindle their faith in God and each other.
- ...someone discover practical ways to make time for what matters most.

- ...another couple experience deeper connection through shared devotions.

Your story matters. By taking just a moment to share how this book has influenced your journey, you will be a source of light and hope for others.

Leave your review here:

Thank you for sharing your voice and helping other couples grow in their love and faith.

Blessings,

The team at Biblical Teachings

27

ALIGNING OUR PARENTING APPROACH

> *"Fathers, do not exasperate your children; instead, bring them up in the training and instruction of the Lord."*
>
> — EPHESIANS 6:4

Parenting is one of the most rewarding but challenging parts of marriage, especially when you and your spouse don't always agree. Differences in how to discipline, set boundaries, or guide your children can create tension if not handled carefully. However, these differences also offer a chance to grow closer as a couple by learning to align your parenting approach.

I remember a time when my spouse and I had different views on how to handle a situation with one of our kids. It was a tough moment, and emotions were high. During that time, I thought of the song *Lean on Me* by Bill Withers, especially the line, *"For it won't be long 'til I'm gonna need somebody to lean on."* It reminded me of the importance of leaning on each other, especially during difficult times. In parenting, just like in other areas of life, it's important to rely on each other's strengths, wisdom, and love to find a path that respects both of our perspectives.

When we face disagreements, it's crucial to pause, listen to each other's concerns, and find a solution that honors both viewpoints. Our goal is to make sure our parenting approach reflects the values we want to pass on to our children.

One of the best ways to align your parenting approach is through open and ongoing communication. Take time to talk about your parenting goals, values, and the areas where you might not see eye to eye. These discussions should be filled with mutual respect and a willingness to compromise when needed. By doing this, you create a united front that not only strengthens your marriage but also provides consistency and stability for your children.

Next Steps

1. **Communicate Regularly:** Make it a habit to check in with each other about your parenting decisions and any concerns you have. Regular communication prevents misunderstandings and helps you stay aligned.
2. **Respect Each Other's Views:** Recognize that both of you bring valuable perspectives to parenting. Approach disagreements with an open mind, and be willing to find common ground.
3. **Seek Unity in Faith:** Let your shared faith guide your parenting decisions. When both of you are committed to the same spiritual principles, it's easier to stay aligned in how you raise your children.

Real Talk

- How do we handle disagreements about parenting, and what can we do to be more aligned?
- What are some key values and principles we want to agree on as we guide our children?

Short Prayer

Lord, thank You for the blessing of being parents. Help us to approach our disagreements with grace, respect, and love. Guide us as we seek to align our parenting approach with Your will, and give us the wisdom to raise our children in a way that honors You. Amen.

28

BRINGING FAITH INTO FAMILY TIME

> *"Let the message of Christ dwell among you richly as you teach and admonish one another with all wisdom through psalms, hymns, and songs from the Spirit, singing to God with gratitude in your hearts."*
>
> — COLOSSIANS 3:16

Integrating faith into our family life is about more than just setting aside time for devotions. It's about making faith a natural part of our everyday interactions and activities. While formal devotions are important, we can also bring faith into family time through small, meaningful moments woven into our daily routines.

I remember reading about a tradition where families bless each other before bedtime, a simple practice that ends the day with gratitude and prayer. This made me think about other easy ways to incorporate faith into our lives. Whether it's saying a prayer together before meals, discussing a lesson that relates to something we're going through, or reflecting on the values behind a family decision, these small actions create a strong foundation of faith for our family.

Faith isn't just something we practice on Sundays; it can guide our everyday lives, including our time together as a family. When we bring faith into our daily activities, we show our children that our beliefs are central to how we live.

One way we've done this is by making gratitude a regular part of our conversations. Whether at the dinner table or during a walk, we often ask each other what we're thankful for that day. This simple practice not only keeps us focused on our blessings but also leads to deeper conversations about how we see faith in our lives. We've also found that using stories from our favorite books or games helps bring faith-based values to life in a way that resonates with our kids.

Next Steps

1. **Weave Faith into Daily Routines:** Look for natural opportunities to talk about your faith during everyday activities. This could be through prayers, gratitude practices, or discussing how biblical principles apply to your daily life.
2. **Create New Traditions:** Consider introducing small faith-based traditions, like saying a blessing before bed or sharing what you're grateful for at the dinner table.
3. **Connect Faith to Interests:** Use your family's favorite activities, whether it's reading, playing games, or spending time outdoors, to discuss faith-based lessons and values.

Real Talk

- How can we integrate faith into our daily family activities beyond traditional devotional time?
- What new practices or traditions can we start to make our faith more present in our everyday life?

Short Prayer

Lord, thank You for the gift of family and the opportunities we have to grow together in faith. Help us to bring Your message into our daily lives, so that every moment can be a reflection of Your love and grace. Guide us as we seek to integrate faith into all that we do, making it a natural and joyful part of our family time. Amen.

Parenting and Family Life

Pause & Reflect

How can we be more intentional in co-parenting to create a faith-centered home for our children?

_____
_____
_____
_____
_____
_____
_____
_____
_____
_____

Plan & Promise

What's one step we can take this week to better model faith and values in our parenting?

_____
_____
_____
_____
_____
_____
_____
_____

Create & Connect

Choose a family worship song that reflects the values you want to instill in your children. Listen to or sing it together, then discuss and write below how the song's message connects with your family's faith journey.

When we walk in faith as a family, we not only guide our children—we create a legacy of love, trust, and devotion that lasts a lifetime.

29

SUPPORTING EACH OTHER THROUGH STRESS

"Do not be anxious about anything, but in every situation, by prayer and petition, with thanksgiving, present your requests to God. And the peace of God, which transcends all understanding, will guard your hearts and your minds in Christ Jesus."

— PHILIPPIANS 4:6-7

Stress is an inevitable part of life, and how we handle it can greatly impact our relationship. During tough times, it's easy to become focused on our own worries and forget that our spouse may be going through similar struggles. However, facing stress together—supporting and encouraging each other—can strengthen your bond and bring you closer as a couple.

It's important to first recognize how each of you typically cope with stress. Some people need to talk through their problems, while others might prefer some quiet time to think things through. Understanding your spouse's needs is key to providing the right kind of support. For example, if your spouse is someone who benefits from talking things out, be ready to listen without immediately trying to fix the problem. On the other hand, if they need space, respect that need and give them time to process their thoughts.

One of the best ways to support each other through stress is by being present and attentive. Small gestures, like asking how your spouse is feeling, offering to help with tasks, or simply being there to listen, can make a big difference. Sometimes, just knowing that someone is there for you is enough to alleviate some of the stress.

Communication is also vital. Regularly check in with each other, especially during particularly stressful periods. Be honest about what you're experiencing and how your spouse can help. This openness fosters a sense of partnership, reminding both of you that you're in this together. Remember that prayer is a powerful tool as well—praying together can bring a sense of peace and unity, allowing both of you to lean on God's strength during difficult times.

Next Steps

1. **Understand Each Other's Coping Styles:** Take time to learn how each of you deals with stress. Use this understanding to provide the support your spouse needs, whether that's space, a listening ear, or practical help.
2. **Communicate Openly:** Keep the lines of communication open, especially during tough times. Share your concerns and listen to each other without judgment or impatience.
3. **Pray Together:** Make prayer a part of your stress management strategy. Praying together invites God's peace into your hearts and helps you face challenges with faith and unity.

Real Talk

- How do we typically cope with stress, and how can we support each other better during tough times?
- What specific actions can we take to help each other when stress levels are high?

Short Prayer

Lord, we thank You for being our source of strength and peace in every situation. Help us to support each other through life's stresses, with patience, understanding, and love. Teach us to turn to You in prayer and to lean on each other as we navigate challenges together. Amen.

30

TURNING TO PRAYER IN HARD TIMES

"Cast all your anxiety on Him because He cares for you."

— 1 PETER 5:7

When life becomes difficult, it's easy to feel overwhelmed and unsure of where to turn. For me, prayer has always been a source of comfort and strength during those times. It's a way to connect with God, to unload my worries, and to seek His guidance. But I've realized that in the busyness and stress of hard times, prayer can sometimes become an afterthought rather than my first response.

I remember a season when everything seemed to be falling apart. The stress was piling up, and I found myself trying to handle it all on my own. It wasn't until I reached a breaking point that I remembered the power of prayer. I decided to bring everything before God, to be honest about my fears and frustrations, and to ask for His help. In those moments of prayer, I felt a peace that I hadn't felt in a long time—a reminder that I didn't have to carry these burdens alone.

Prayer isn't just about asking God for help, though that's certainly part of it. It's also about aligning our hearts with His will, finding peace in His presence, and trusting that He's working even when we can't see it. The more I turn to prayer in difficult times, the more I see its power to shift my perspective. It helps me to let go of control, to trust that God is in charge, and to focus on what truly matters.

To make prayer more central in my life, especially during hard times, I've started incorporating it into my daily routine. Whether it's a quick prayer in the morning, a moment of gratitude at the end of the day, or simply pausing to pray when stress hits, these small steps make a big difference. I've also found that praying with my spouse brings us closer together and helps us face challenges as a united front.

Next Steps

1. **Make Prayer a Habit:** Incorporate prayer into your daily routine, so it becomes your natural response to challenges. Whether it's a set time each day or simply praying whenever you feel anxious, consistency is key.
2. **Pray Together:** If you're married, pray with your spouse. There's power in coming together before God, seeking His guidance and strength as a couple.
3. **Let Go and Trust:** Use prayer as an opportunity to release your worries to God. Trust that He's in control, and let His peace guard your heart and mind.

Real Talk

- What role does prayer play when you face challenges, and how can you make it more central?
- How can we remind ourselves to turn to prayer first rather than as a last resort?

Short Prayer

Lord, thank You for being our refuge and strength in times of trouble. Help us to turn to You in prayer, trusting in Your care and finding peace in Your presence. May prayer be our first response in every situation, and may we grow closer to You as we rely on Your guidance and love. Amen.

31

BALANCING INDIVIDUAL NEEDS & SHARED RESPONSIBILITIES

"Carry each other's burdens, and in this way you will fulfill the law of Christ."

— GALATIANS 6:2

Balancing individual needs with shared responsibilities is a common challenge in relationships. Every couple faces the delicate task of ensuring that each person's personal needs are met while also taking care of the responsibilities they share. Whether it's managing a household, raising children, or maintaining a relationship, finding this balance is key to a healthy partnership.

It's a bit like the metaphor in *Friends*, where Ross says, *"We were on a break!"*—emphasizing how miscommunication and unmet needs can cause tension in a relationship. Just as Ross and Rachel had to navigate their own needs and desires while trying to stay connected, couples today must balance their personal time and interests with the demands of shared responsibilities. The goal is to ensure that both partners feel supported, respected, and valued, without losing sight of their individual identities.

Couples can start by having open and honest conversations about what they need individually—whether it's alone time, pursuing a hobby, or maintaining friendships outside the relationship. At the same time, it's important to discuss how they can work together to manage their shared responsibilities. This might mean dividing household chores, coordinating schedules to support each other's goals, or setting aside quality time for their relationship amidst their busy lives.

The key is to approach these conversations with understanding and flexibility. It's about recognizing that your partner's needs are just as important as your own and finding ways to support each other in those needs. By doing so, couples can build a partnership that honors both their individuality and their commitment to each other.

Next Steps

1. **Communicate Your Needs:** Make it a habit to check in with each other about your individual needs and how they can be met without neglecting shared responsibilities.
2. **Divide Responsibilities Fairly:** Work together to divide household chores, parenting duties, and other responsibilities in a way that feels fair and balanced to both of you.
3. **Prioritize Quality Time:** Ensure that your individual pursuits don't come at the expense of your relationship. Set aside time regularly to reconnect and nurture your partnership.

Real Talk

- How do we balance our individual needs with our shared responsibilities?
- What adjustments can we make to ensure both of us feel supported and valued in our relationship?

Short Prayer

Lord, thank You for the partnership we share. Help us to balance our individual needs with our responsibilities to each other. Guide us in understanding, patience, and love as we navigate this balance, so that our relationship may grow stronger and reflect Your grace. Amen.

32

IDENTIFYING & ADDRESSING STRESS TRIGGERS

"Anxiety weighs down the heart, but a kind word cheers it up."

— PROVERBS 12:25

Stress is a part of life, but when it's left unaddressed, it can really impact our well-being and relationships. Over time, I've learned that the first step in managing stress is understanding what triggers it. Whether it's a heavy workload, financial pressures, or even having too many social commitments, pinpointing these triggers allows me to take proactive steps to address them before they become overwhelming.

One thing that has really made a difference for me is recognizing the patterns in my stress. For instance, I've noticed that when I take on too much, I start to feel anxious and irritable. By acknowledging this pattern, I can take steps to simplify my schedule or ask for help before the stress builds up. This not only helps me manage my own stress but also prevents it from affecting my relationships with those around me.

Talking openly with my spouse about our stress triggers has also been incredibly beneficial. We've realized that we each have different things that stress us out, and by sharing these with each other, we can better support one another. Sometimes, it's as simple as taking over a task when the other person feels overwhelmed, or just being there to listen when one of us needs to vent. By addressing our stress triggers together, we're able to face challenges as a team rather than letting stress create distance between us.

In addition to these conversations, we've also started to implement small changes in our daily routine that help reduce stress. Whether it's setting aside quiet time in the morning, going for a walk together in the evening, or just making sure we have a few minutes to check in with each other every day, these small adjustments make a big difference. By tackling stress together and being mindful of what triggers it, we've found that we can keep our relationship strong even during life's more challenging moments.

Next Steps

1. **Identify Your Triggers:** Take time to reflect on what specifically causes you stress. It might be certain situations, deadlines, or even interactions that weigh on you.
2. **Communicate Openly:** Share your stress triggers with your spouse and listen to theirs. Understanding each other's stressors allows you to be more supportive and empathetic.
3. **Create a Plan:** Work together to develop strategies for managing stress, whether it's through better time management, setting boundaries, or practicing relaxation techniques.

Real Talk

- What are your stress triggers, and how can you address them together?
- How can we support each other better when stress arises?

Short Prayer

Lord, thank You for being our source of peace and comfort in times of stress. Help us to recognize and address the things that weigh us down, and give us the wisdom to support each other through life's challenges. May our partnership be strengthened as we lean on You and on each other. Amen.

Handling Stress & Life Challenges

Pause & Reflect

How can we support each other better when life gets stressful?

Plan & Promise

What's one specific action we can take this week to help each other manage stress more effectively?

Create & Connect

Create a list of your personal stress triggers and discuss them with each other. Work together to brainstorm ways to manage or reduce these triggers in your day-to-day life.

Facing life's challenges together strengthens the bond between us, reminding us that we're not alone—we have each other and God by our side.

33

CELEBRATING OUR MILESTONES

"The Lord has done great things for us, and we are filled with joy."

— PSALM 126:3

Celebrating milestones in our relationship is more than just marking time—it's about cherishing the growth, love, and commitment that have brought us to this point. Whether it's an anniversary, a special achievement, or even a small victory in our journey together, these moments are opportunities to pause, reflect, and rejoice in what we've accomplished as a couple.

I've found that the most meaningful celebrations aren't always the grand ones; often, it's the personal and thoughtful gestures that mean the most. It's like in the song *Thinking Out Loud* by Ed Sheeran, where he sings, *"We found love right where we are."* It's a reminder that the most special moments don't require a big production—they happen when we're simply being present with each other. For us, it's the quiet dinner where we reminisce about our journey, the handwritten notes expressing our gratitude, or the spontaneous decision to revisit the place where we first met. These simple yet intentional acts remind us of the love and effort we've poured into our relationship and how far we've come.

Over time, we've made it a priority to be intentional about how we celebrate our milestones. Instead of just going through the motions, we take time to reflect on what each milestone means to us and how we can honor it in a way that feels true to our bond. Sometimes it's a small getaway, and other times it's a heartfelt conversation about our hopes for the future. No matter how we choose to celebrate, the goal is always the same: to strengthen our connection and express our gratitude for the journey we've shared.

Next Steps

1. **Be Intentional:** Take time to plan how you'll celebrate each milestone. Think about what makes your relationship special and incorporate those elements into your celebration.
2. **Reflect Together:** Use these occasions to talk about your journey as a couple—what you've learned, how you've grown, and what you're looking forward to. This reflection can deepen your connection and appreciation for each other.
3. **Create New Traditions:** Consider starting a new tradition that you can look forward to each year, whether it's revisiting a favorite place, writing letters to each other, or dedicating a day to do something meaningful together.

Real Talk

- How do we celebrate our relationship milestones and make those celebrations more meaningful?
- What are some new traditions or activities we can start to honor our journey together?

Short Prayer

Lord, thank You for the journey we've shared and the milestones we've reached together. Help us to celebrate these moments with gratitude and joy, always remembering that it is by Your grace that we continue to grow in love. May our celebrations be a reflection of our commitment to each other and to You. Amen.

34

REFLECTING ON OUR GROWTH

> *"Because of the Lord's great love we are not consumed, for his compassions never fail. They are new every morning; great is your faithfulness."*
>
> — LAMENTATIONS 3:22-23

Reflecting on growth as a couple is an essential practice that helps deepen understanding, strengthen bonds, and set the stage for continued progress in the relationship. Over the past year, every couple experiences both challenges and triumphs, and taking time to look back on these moments can reveal how far they've come together. This reflection not only celebrates growth but also fosters gratitude and a renewed commitment to the journey ahead.

For couples, reflection can begin by revisiting significant moments from the past year—both the highs and the lows. This might include discussing how they handled a difficult situation, how they supported each other through a major life event, or how they celebrated a personal or shared accomplishment. Each of these moments provides insight into how they've grown individually and as a unit.

Another way to reflect on growth is through open dialogue about what they've learned from each other over the past year. Couples can share specific examples of how they've become more patient, loving, or understanding. This conversation can also highlight areas where they've grown stronger together, such as improving communication, building trust, or learning to compromise.

Finally, couples can reflect on their spiritual growth by considering how their faith has played a role in their relationship. They can discuss how they've leaned on their faith during tough times, how prayer or devotionals have brought them closer, or how they've seen God's hand in their journey together.

Next Steps

1. **Review Key Moments:** Set aside time to look back on the year's significant events. Discuss what went well, what was challenging, and how those experiences contributed to your growth.
2. **Share Lessons Learned:** Talk about the lessons each of you has learned over the past year. Focus on how these lessons have made you stronger individually and as a couple.
3. **Acknowledge Spiritual Growth:** Reflect on how your faith has influenced your relationship. Consider how your spiritual practices have helped you navigate the year's challenges and joys.

Real Talk

- What are some ways we can reflect on our growth over the past year?
- How have we changed, both individually and as a couple, and what can we learn from those changes?

Short Prayer

Lord, thank You for Your faithfulness throughout this past year. Help us to see the growth You have nurtured in us as a couple. Guide us as we reflect on our journey, and give us the wisdom to carry forward the lessons we've learned. May our hearts be filled with gratitude for Your love and grace. Amen.

35

SETTING NEW GOALS TOGETHER

"Brothers and sisters, I do not consider myself yet to have taken hold of it. But one thing I do: Forgetting what is behind and straining toward what is ahead, I press on toward the goal to win the prize for which God has called me heavenward in Christ Jesus."

— PHILIPPIANS 3:13-14

Setting goals together as a couple is a powerful way to keep your relationship growing and moving forward. It's a chance to look back on what you've already achieved and to dream about what's next. Whether it's something big, like buying a home, or something smaller, like starting a new daily routine, these milestones are worth celebrating. But just as important is the process of setting new goals that will continue to challenge and inspire you both.

Take some time to reflect on the goals you've already reached together. What did it take to get there? What did you learn from the experience? Looking back at these successes can give you valuable insights into how you work best as a team and what strengths you bring to the table. It's also a great opportunity to celebrate the hard work and commitment you both put into making these goals a reality.

As you think about the future, consider what new goals you want to set together. These goals could be related to your personal growth, your relationship, your family, or your spiritual journey. The important thing is to choose goals that align with your shared values and excite you both. Setting these goals isn't just about hitting targets; it's about deepening your connection by dreaming and planning for your future together.

This process of setting and achieving goals together strengthens your bond, as it helps you stay focused on what matters most to both of you. It also keeps your relationship dynamic and full of purpose, ensuring that you continue to grow and evolve as a couple.

Next Steps

1. **Reflect on Achievements:** Take time to acknowledge the goals you've accomplished together. Discuss what worked well and how those achievements have strengthened your relationship.
2. **Set New Goals:** Identify new goals that inspire both of you. These can be related to various aspects of your life, such as your relationship, personal growth, career, or spiritual life.
3. **Plan Together:** Once you've set your goals, create a plan for how you'll achieve them. Be sure to support each other along the way and celebrate the progress you make.

Real Talk

- What goals have we achieved together, and how have they impacted our relationship?
- What new goals can we set for the future, and how can we work together to achieve them?

Short Prayer

Lord, thank You for the journey we've shared and the goals we've achieved together. Guide us as we set new goals for our future, and give us the wisdom and determination to pursue them with faith and love. Help us to support and encourage each other every step of the way. Amen.

36

MAKING GRATITUDE A HABIT

"And whatever you do, whether in word or deed, do it all in the name of the Lord Jesus, giving thanks to God the Father through him."

— COLOSSIANS 3:17

Gratitude is one of the simplest yet most powerful ways to strengthen our relationship. When we regularly express appreciation for each other, it not only lifts our spirits but also deepens our connection. However, it's easy to let this practice slip in the busyness of everyday life. I've learned that making gratitude a habit takes intentionality, but the rewards are well worth the effort.

In our relationship, expressing gratitude doesn't always have to be about grand gestures. Sometimes, it's the small, everyday acknowledgments that mean the most. A simple "thank you" for making dinner, or a note left on the mirror expressing appreciation for a thoughtful gesture, can go a long way. These little moments of gratitude remind us that we're seen, valued, and loved.

To make gratitude a consistent habit, we've started incorporating it into our daily routine. For instance, we've made it a point to share one thing we're thankful for about each other at the end of each day. This practice not only keeps gratitude at the forefront of our minds but also encourages us to notice and appreciate the small things that might otherwise go unrecognized. Over time, these expressions of gratitude build up, creating a positive atmosphere in our relationship where love and appreciation thrive.

Making gratitude a habit requires conscious effort, but it's one that pays off in both small and significant ways. It shifts our focus from what's lacking to what's abundant, from frustrations to blessings. As we continue to practice gratitude, we find that it strengthens our bond, fosters a spirit of thankfulness, and reminds us of the love and commitment we share.

Next Steps

1. **Start Small:** Begin by expressing gratitude for the little things. Make it a point to acknowledge even the smallest acts of kindness or thoughtfulness.
2. **Create a Routine:** Find a time each day to share what you're thankful for about each other. Whether it's over dinner, before bed, or in a morning conversation, make it a regular part of your day.
3. **Keep It Genuine:** Let your expressions of gratitude come from the heart. Whether it's a note, a word of thanks, or a small gesture, make sure it reflects your true appreciation.

Real Talk

- How do we currently express gratitude for each other, and how can we make it more of a habit?
- What are some specific ways we can show appreciation daily?

Short Prayer

Lord, thank You for the gift of gratitude and the way it draws us closer to each other. Help us to make gratitude a daily habit, reminding us to appreciate the love and blessings we share. May our expressions of thanks be a reflection of Your goodness in our lives. Amen.

Celebrating Milestones & Achievements

Pause & Reflect

How have we grown as a couple, and what milestones can we celebrate together?

Plan & Promise

What's one meaningful way we can celebrate our next milestone, big or small, together?

Create & Connect

Take time to look back on past anniversaries or special moments. Write down how each event shaped your relationship and discuss what you've learned from those experiences.

_____
_____
_____
_____
_____
_____
_____
_____
_____
_____
_____
_____
_____
_____
_____
_____
_____
_____
_____
_____

Every milestone is a reminder of how far we've come, and every celebration strengthens the bond we share.

37

THE ROLE OF FORGIVENESS IN OUR MARRIAGE

> *"For if you forgive other people when they sin against you, your heavenly Father will also forgive you. But if you do not forgive others their sins, your Father will not forgive your sins."*
>
> — MATTHEW 6:14-15

Forgiveness is a cornerstone of any healthy marriage. No matter how much love and care you put into your relationship, misunderstandings, hurt feelings, and mistakes are inevitable. It's in these moments that forgiveness becomes crucial, allowing you to heal, move forward, and grow stronger as a couple.

Forgiveness in marriage isn't just about letting go of a specific incident; it's about choosing to prioritize your relationship over the pain. It's an act of grace that reflects the forgiveness we receive from God. When you forgive each other, you acknowledge the imperfections that exist in both of you and make a conscious decision to move forward without holding on to bitterness or resentment.

Practicing forgiveness more readily involves a few key steps. First, it's important to communicate openly about the hurt and to listen without defensiveness. Understanding each other's perspectives helps to clear the air and paves the way for genuine reconciliation. Second, try to approach forgiveness with humility. Remember that both of you have likely been on both sides of needing to forgive and be forgiven. This mutual understanding fosters compassion and makes it easier to offer grace when it's needed most.

Finally, it's essential to let go of the desire to revisit past grievances. True forgiveness means not bringing up old wounds during future disagreements. Instead, focus on building trust and strengthening your bond through love and understanding. The more you practice forgiveness, the more resilient your marriage will become.

Next Steps

1. **Communicate Openly:** Discuss the hurt with honesty and listen to each other's feelings without interrupting or defending. This creates a safe space for healing and understanding.
2. **Approach with Humility:** Remember that both of you are imperfect and in need of grace. Approach forgiveness with a spirit of humility and compassion.
3. **Release the Past:** Once forgiveness is given, commit to not revisiting past grievances. Focus on moving forward and rebuilding trust.

Real Talk

- What role does forgiveness play in our relationship, and how can we practice it more readily?
- How can we create an environment where forgiveness is given and received with love and understanding?

Short Prayer

Lord, thank You for the gift of forgiveness and the example You have set for us. Help us to forgive each other as You forgive us, with love, grace, and humility. Teach us to let go of past hurts and to focus on building a stronger, more loving relationship. Amen.

38

EXTENDING GRACE TO EACH OTHER

"Bear with each other and forgive one another if any of you has a grievance against someone. Forgive as the Lord forgave you."

— COLOSSIANS 3:13

Extending grace in marriage is essential because, despite our best efforts, we all fall short at times. Whether it's forgetting an important date, saying something we didn't mean, or simply being too tired to be our best selves, there are moments when we let each other down. How we respond to these moments defines the strength and depth of our relationship. Grace is what bridges the gap between our imperfections and our desire to love each other well.

One of the best examples of extending grace can be found in the TV show *Parks and Recreation*. Ben and Leslie, two characters who love each other deeply, frequently navigate their differences with grace and humor. Even when they disagree or make mistakes, they choose to support and forgive each other, prioritizing their relationship over their frustrations. This approach reminds me that extending grace isn't just about overlooking flaws; it's about choosing love, even when it's difficult.

In our own marriage, I've learned that extending grace often means pausing before reacting. When my spouse falls short, my first instinct might be to get upset or point out the mistake. But instead, I try to remember the many times I've needed grace and how much it meant when it was given to me. By taking a deep breath and responding with understanding, I can offer the same kindness that I've received.

Improving how we extend grace to each other starts with empathy. It's about putting ourselves in our spouse's shoes and considering how they're feeling and what they might need in that moment. It's also about letting go of the need to always be right and instead focusing on what's best for the relationship. When we prioritize grace, we create a safe space where love can grow, even in the face of mistakes.

Next Steps

1. **Practice Empathy:** Before reacting, take a moment to consider your spouse's perspective. This can help you respond with compassion rather than frustration.
2. **Focus on the Bigger Picture:** Remember that your relationship is more important than any one mistake. Choose to prioritize love and understanding over being right.
3. **Forgive Quickly:** Don't hold onto grudges. The sooner you extend grace, the sooner you can move forward together.

Real Talk

- How do we extend grace to each other when we fall short, and what can we do to improve?
- What are some ways we can remind ourselves to prioritize grace in our relationship?

Short Prayer

Lord, thank You for the grace You extend to us each day. Help us to offer that same grace to each other, especially when we fall short. Teach us to respond with love, understanding, and compassion, and to prioritize our relationship above all else. Amen.

39

FORGIVING & MOVING FORWARD TOGETHER

"Get rid of all bitterness, rage and anger, brawling and slander, along with every form of malice. Be kind and compassionate to one another, forgiving each other, just as in Christ God forgave you."

— EPHESIANS 4:31-32

Forgiveness can be challenging, especially when both of us are feeling hurt. In those moments, it's easy to hold onto our pain and wait for the other person to make the first move. But I've learned that holding onto hurt only deepens the divide between us. If we want to move forward together, someone has to take the first step toward reconciliation, and often that starts with initiating forgiveness.

When both of us are hurt, it's important to acknowledge the pain we're each experiencing. Instead of focusing on who's right or wrong, we need to create space for understanding. This means listening to each other's feelings without interrupting or defending ourselves. By truly hearing each other out, we can start to break down the walls that hurt has built between us.

Initiating forgiveness doesn't mean minimizing the pain or brushing it aside. It means recognizing that the relationship is more important than the conflict. I've found that when I approach my spouse with a heart ready to forgive, it opens the door for healing and restoration. It's not about winning or losing but about choosing to prioritize our love over our differences.

Moving forward together requires more than just words; it requires action. After we've forgiven each other, we need to take intentional steps to rebuild trust and restore our connection. This might involve making small changes in how we communicate, setting aside quality time to reconnect, or even seeking guidance through prayer or counseling. The goal is to ensure that we're not just moving past the hurt but growing stronger because of it.

Next Steps

1. **Listen First:** Make space for each other to express your hurt without interrupting or defending yourself. Understanding each other's pain is the first step toward healing.
2. **Prioritize the Relationship:** Remember that your relationship is more important than the conflict. Approach forgiveness with a heart focused on reconciliation, not on winning or losing.
3. **Take Action Together:** After forgiving each other, commit to taking steps that will strengthen your relationship moving forward. This could include better communication, more quality time, or seeking support if needed.

Real Talk

- How can we initiate forgiveness when both of us feel hurt, and how do we move forward together?
- What specific steps can we take to rebuild trust and strengthen our connection after a conflict?

Short Prayer

Lord, thank You for Your endless forgiveness and grace. Help us to forgive each other as You have forgiven us. Teach us to let go of our hurts and to prioritize our relationship above all else. Guide us as we move forward together, strengthening our bond and growing in love. Amen.

40

REMINDING EACH OTHER OF GOD'S GRACE

"But he said to me, 'My grace is sufficient for you, for my power is made perfect in weakness."

— 2 CORINTHIANS 12:9

In the day-to-day busyness of life, it's easy for couples to lose sight of the constant presence of God's grace. Yet, God's grace is a source of strength, comfort, and renewal for every believer, and reminding each other of this truth can be incredibly powerful in a marriage. Whether you're facing challenges or simply navigating the ordinary routines of life, consistently bringing each other back to the reality of God's grace can help deepen your spiritual connection and strengthen your bond.

One simple way to remind each other of God's grace is by speaking words of encouragement rooted in Scripture. When one person is feeling overwhelmed or discouraged, the other can gently remind them that God's grace is sufficient for every need. This can be as simple as sharing a verse, offering a prayer, or even just acknowledging the ways God has been faithful in the past. These reminders can shift focus from the difficulties at hand to the greater truth of God's unchanging love and support.

Another way to keep God's grace at the forefront is by creating small, daily rituals that highlight it. This could involve beginning or ending the day with a prayer of gratitude, acknowledging God's grace in all circumstances, or taking moments throughout the day to reflect on where His grace has shown up in your lives. By doing this, couples can cultivate an ongoing awareness of God's presence and provision, helping them to stay grounded in His grace no matter what they face.

Finally, it's important to model grace to each other. Just as God shows us grace in our imperfections, couples can mirror that by extending grace to one another in their daily interactions. Whether it's offering forgiveness quickly, being patient when one person is stressed, or supporting each other through personal struggles, these acts of grace not only strengthen the relationship but also serve as a living reminder of God's grace at work in your lives.

Next Steps

1. **Share Encouragement:** Regularly remind each other of God's promises and the sufficiency of His grace, especially during challenging times.
2. **Create Grace-Centered Rituals:** Establish daily habits that focus on recognizing and celebrating God's grace in your lives.
3. **Model Grace:** Be intentional about showing grace to each other in your words and actions, reflecting God's love and patience in your relationship.

Real Talk

- How can we remind each other of God's grace in our daily lives?
- What practices can we incorporate to keep God's grace central in our relationship?

Short Prayer

Lord, thank You for Your amazing grace that sustains us each day. Help us to remind each other of this grace continually, especially in moments of weakness or difficulty. Teach us to live in a way that reflects Your love and to support each other with the same grace You have shown us. Amen.

Forgiveness and Grace

Pause & Reflect

How can we practice forgiveness and extend grace to each other more freely in our marriage?

Plan & Promise

What's one step we can take this week to forgive past hurts and move forward with grace?

Create & Connect

Each partner writes a letter to the other, expressing forgiveness for past mistakes and a commitment to moving forward with love and understanding.

True love means forgiving each other as God forgives us, offering grace even when it's difficult, and choosing to move forward in unity and trust.

41

STAYING CONSISTENT IN OUR FAITH

"Never be lacking in zeal, but keep your spiritual fervor, serving the Lord."

— ROMANS 12:11

Staying consistent in your faith practices can be challenging, especially when life gets busy or obstacles arise. Whether it's the demands of work, family responsibilities, or simply feeling too tired, it's easy to let your spiritual habits slip. Yet, just like maintaining any good habit, staying consistent in your faith requires intention, commitment, and sometimes a bit of creativity.

Think about how maintaining a routine is portrayed in the show *The Office*. Dwight Schrute famously says, *"Before I do anything, I ask myself, 'Would an idiot do that?' And if the answer is yes, I do not do that thing."* While Dwight's approach is humorous, it speaks to the idea of being intentional and consistent in our actions, even when it's difficult. In the same way, staying consistent in your faith practices—whether it's daily prayer, Bible reading, or attending church—requires deliberate choices that prioritize your spiritual growth, even when it's easier to skip them.

One of the biggest obstacles to consistency in faith is simply the busyness of life. Between work, family, and other commitments, finding time for God can feel like just another item on an already full to-do list. Overcoming this requires viewing your faith not as an obligation but as a source of strength and renewal. Consider integrating your faith practices into your existing routines. For example, listen to a devotional podcast during your commute, or set aside a few minutes before bed to reflect on the day and pray together. Small adjustments can make a big difference in staying consistent.

Another challenge might be spiritual dryness—times when you feel disconnected from God or less motivated to engage in spiritual practices. During these periods, it's important to remember that faith isn't based on feelings alone. Keep going through the motions, trusting that God is with you even when you don't feel His presence as strongly. Sometimes, simply showing up—whether it's to church, prayer, or Bible study—can help rekindle your spiritual fervor.

Next Steps

1. **Identify Your Obstacles:** Take time to discuss the specific obstacles that have kept you from staying consistent in your faith. Understanding these challenges is the first step to overcoming them.
2. **Adjust Your Routines:** Find creative ways to incorporate faith practices into your daily life. Whether it's through prayer, reading, or serving, consistency is key.
3. **Lean on Each Other:** Encourage and support one another in staying consistent. Accountability can help you both stay focused on your spiritual goals.

Real Talk

- What obstacles have kept us from staying consistent in our faith practices, and how can we overcome them?
- How can we adjust our routines to make room for regular spiritual practices?

Short Prayer

Lord, thank You for the gift of faith and the strength it brings to our lives. Help us to overcome the obstacles that keep us from staying consistent in our spiritual practices. Give us the wisdom and discipline to make our faith a central part of our daily lives. Amen.

42

KEEPING EACH OTHER ACCOUNTABLE

> *"And let us consider how we may spur one another on toward love and good deeds, not giving up meeting together, as some are in the habit of doing, but encouraging one another—and all the more as you see the Day approaching."*
>
> — HEBREWS 10:24-25

Helping each other stay on track in your spiritual journey is important, but it should feel encouraging, not like added pressure. The goal is to grow together in faith, supporting each other in a way that strengthens both your relationship with God and with each other.

One simple way to do this is by setting spiritual goals together. These could be things like praying together every day, attending church regularly, or reading a devotional each week. When you both have the same goals, it's easier to stay motivated and focused. Talk openly about what you want to achieve and agree on how you'll help each other reach those goals.

Communication is key. Regularly check in with each other about how you're doing, not just to make sure you're sticking to your goals, but also to share what you're learning, where you're growing, and even where you might be struggling. Approach these talks with kindness and a desire to grow together, rather than as a task that needs to be done. This keeps the focus on supporting each other rather than just completing a list.

It's also important to be patient and understanding. There will be times when life gets busy or one of you feels less connected to your faith. When that happens, gently remind each other of the goals you've set, but also be forgiving and supportive. Remember, the purpose of keeping each other accountable is to help each other grow, not to create stress or pressure.

Next Steps

1. **Set Shared Goals:** Find spiritual goals you can work on together, like praying daily or reading Scripture. This helps you stay accountable without feeling stressed.
2. **Talk Regularly:** Make time to talk about how your spiritual journey is going. Share what's working, what's not, and how you can help each other.
3. **Be Patient:** If one of you falls behind, respond with understanding. Your goal is to help each other grow, not to add pressure.

Real Talk

- How can we keep each other accountable in our spiritual journey without feeling pressured?
- What specific goals can we set together to help us grow in our faith while supporting each other?

Short Prayer

Lord, thank You for giving us the chance to walk this spiritual journey together. Help us to encourage each other with love, patience, and kindness as we grow in our faith. Guide us as we set goals together and give us the strength to keep each other on track. Amen.

43

BUILDING FAITH-CENTERED ROUTINES

"These commandments that I give you today are to be on your hearts. Impress them on your children. Talk about them when you sit at home and when you walk along the road, when you lie down and when you get up."

— DEUTERONOMY 6:6-7

Building routines that keep our faith at the center of our lives has been essential for us. With so many demands and distractions, it's easy to let our spiritual practices slip. But by establishing small, consistent rituals, we can make sure that our faith remains a priority, guiding our daily actions and strengthening our relationship with each other and with God.

One of the routines that has made a difference for us is starting and ending each day with prayer. In the morning, we take a few minutes to pray together, asking for God's guidance for the day ahead. At night, we close the day by thanking God for His blessings and asking for rest and peace. These simple moments of connection help us to stay grounded in our faith, no matter how busy the day gets.

Another practice we've embraced is reading Scripture together regularly. Whether it's a chapter a day or a weekly study, this routine keeps God's Word fresh in our minds and provides opportunities for meaningful conversations. We also try to incorporate our faith into our everyday activities, like listening to worship music during chores or discussing a Bible verse while on a walk. These small acts remind us that faith isn't just for Sundays—it's a part of every aspect of our lives.

Building these routines doesn't have to be complicated. The key is to find what works for us and to be consistent. Over time, these small rituals become habits that draw us closer to God and to each other.

Next Steps

1. **Start and End the Day with Prayer:** Make it a habit to pray together in the morning and before bed. This keeps your faith at the forefront, no matter what the day brings.
2. **Incorporate Scripture:** Find time to read the Bible together, whether it's a daily verse or a longer study. Discussing Scripture helps keep your focus on God's Word.
3. **Infuse Faith into Daily Activities:** Look for ways to bring your faith into your everyday routines, like listening to worship music or discussing your faith during regular activities.

Real Talk

- What small rituals or routines can we establish to keep our faith at the center of our lives?
- How can we make these routines a consistent part of our daily lives?

Short Prayer

Lord, thank You for the opportunity to build our lives around You. Help us to create and maintain routines that keep our faith at the center of everything we do. May these small practices draw us closer to You and to each other, and may they become a source of strength and comfort in our daily lives. Amen.

44

OVERCOMING OBSTACLES TOGETHER

> *"No temptation has overtaken you except what is common to mankind. And God is faithful; he will not let you be tempted beyond what you can bear. But when you are tempted, he will also provide a way out so that you can endure it."*
>
> — 1 CORINTHIANS 10:13

Every relationship faces obstacles, especially when it comes to maintaining faith practices. Whether it's a busy schedule, stress, or simply feeling distant from God, these challenges can make it hard to stay consistent in our spiritual lives. But just like in any love story, the key to overcoming these obstacles is to face them together, supporting each other along the way.

I'm reminded of the classic love song *Ain't No Mountain High Enough* by Marvin Gaye and Tammi Terrell. The lyrics capture the determination to overcome any barrier for the sake of love. In our faith journey, this same mindset can be applied. No matter what obstacles come our way, we can approach them with the confidence that, together, we can overcome them with God's help.

One of the obstacles we've identified is the challenge of finding time for our faith practices amidst our busy schedules. Life gets hectic, and it's easy to let our spiritual routines slip. To handle this, we've committed to setting aside specific times in our day, even if just for a few minutes, to pray or read Scripture together. By doing this, we create a rhythm that keeps our faith practices intact, no matter how full our calendars get.

Another challenge we've faced is dealing with moments of spiritual dryness, where it feels like God is distant or our faith isn't as vibrant. During these times, we remind each other that faith isn't about emotions but about trust and commitment. We encourage each other to keep going, even when it's hard, knowing that these dry spells are temporary and that God is always with us.

Next Steps

1. **Identify Your Obstacles:** Discuss the specific challenges that hinder your faith practices, whether it's time, stress, or spiritual dryness.
2. **Create a Plan:** Develop a strategy to overcome these obstacles together, such as setting aside specific times for prayer or offering each other encouragement during difficult seasons.
3. **Stay Committed:** Remember that, just like in the song, no obstacle is too big when you face it together. Lean on each other and on God's strength to overcome whatever comes your way.

Real Talk

- What potential obstacles to our faith practices can we identify, and how will we handle them together?
- How can we remind each other of our commitment to these practices, especially when challenges arise?

Short Prayer

Lord, thank You for being our source of strength in every challenge. Help us to identify and overcome the obstacles that hinder our faith practices. Give us the wisdom and perseverance to face these challenges together, trusting in Your guidance and support. Amen.

Maintaining Consistency in Faith Practices

Pause & Reflect

What obstacles have kept us from staying consistent in our faith practices, and how can we overcome them together?

Plan & Promise

What's one small change we can make this week to strengthen our faith routines together?

Create & Connect

Create a visual representation of your faith goals and practices. Use images, words, and drawings that reflect how you want to grow spiritually as a couple. Take a photo of it and paste it in the space below.

Consistency in faith is not about perfection, but about making room for God every day—together, no matter how small the effort.

45

ENCOURAGING PERSONAL & SPIRITUAL GROWTH

"Therefore encourage one another and build each other up, just as in fact you are doing."

— 1 THESSALONIANS 5:11

Encouraging each other's personal and spiritual growth is one of the most meaningful ways to strengthen your relationship. It's about being each other's biggest supporter, cheering each other on as you pursue your goals and deepen your faith. Just like in any good relationship, when you lift each other up, you both grow stronger together.

A great example of this is found in the song *Wind Beneath My Wings* by Bette Midler. The lyrics talk about someone being the quiet support behind the scenes, helping another person reach their full potential. In your relationship, you can be that *"wind"* for each other—helping each other soar higher than you could on your own.

To encourage personal and spiritual growth, start by taking an active interest in each other's goals and passions. Whether it's pursuing a new hobby, advancing in a career, or growing deeper in faith, be intentional about supporting each other. Celebrate successes, provide encouragement during challenges, and be there to listen and offer advice when needed.

In terms of spiritual growth, consider setting goals together that challenge both of you to grow in your faith. This could involve studying a new book of the Bible, volunteering together, or joining a small group. Additionally, encourage each other to pursue individual spiritual practices that resonate with each of you, whether that's prayer, meditation, or reading devotional materials.

Next Steps

1. **Be Each Other's Cheerleader:** Actively support each other's personal and spiritual goals. Celebrate victories and offer encouragement when challenges arise.
2. **Grow Together and Individually:** Set shared spiritual goals, but also respect and encourage each other's individual paths of growth.
3. **Make It a Priority:** Regularly check in on each other's progress and provide the support needed to keep moving forward.

Real Talk

- How do we encourage each other's personal and spiritual growth, and what more can we do?
- What specific goals can we set together to grow both personally and spiritually?

Short Prayer

Lord, thank You for the gift of partnership in both personal and spiritual growth. Help us to be each other's greatest encouragers, lifting each other up as we pursue our goals and deepen our faith. Guide us in building a relationship that reflects Your love and grace, where we inspire each other to grow closer to You every day. Amen.

46

NURTURING EACH OTHER'S TALENTS

"Each of you should use whatever gift you have received to serve others, as faithful stewards of God's grace in its various forms."

— 1 PETER 4:10

Recognizing and nurturing each other's talents and passions is a wonderful way to grow closer as a couple. When you take the time to see and appreciate the unique gifts your partner has, you not only affirm their strengths but also encourage them to use those gifts in meaningful ways. This mutual support helps both of you grow individually and as a team, strengthening your relationship and deepening your bond.

To start nurturing each other's talents, begin by expressing what you admire in your partner. Acknowledge the qualities and passions that make them unique, whether it's their creativity, leadership, compassion, or a specific talent like music, writing, or teaching. When you verbalize your appreciation for these gifts, it shows your partner that you notice and value who they are and what they contribute to your relationship and to the world.

After identifying these talents, think about how you can support each other in developing them. This might mean encouraging your partner to pursue further education or training, giving them the time and space they need to practice, or simply offering words of encouragement as they take steps toward their goals. Additionally, consider how you can incorporate these talents into your shared life, perhaps by working on projects together that make the most of both of your strengths.

By actively supporting and nurturing each other's gifts, you not only help each other grow, but you also create a stronger, more connected partnership. This shared journey of growth and encouragement deepens your love and helps you both become the best versions of yourselves, together.

Next Steps

1. **Recognize Each Other's Gifts:** Take time to acknowledge the talents and passions you see in each other. Share what you admire and appreciate about your partner's unique gifts.
2. **Support Growth:** Encourage each other to develop your talents further. Whether it's through learning, practicing, or simply cheering each other on, make growth a shared priority.
3. **Use Your Gifts Together:** Look for opportunities to combine your talents in ways that serve others and enrich your relationship. Working together can be a powerful way to honor God with the gifts He has given you.

Real Talk

- What talents or passions do we see in each other, and how can we nurture them?
- How can we support each other in using these gifts to serve others and glorify God?

Short Prayer

Lord, thank You for the unique talents and passions You have placed within us. Help us to recognize and nurture these gifts in each other, so that we may use them to serve others and honor You. Guide us as we grow together, supporting each other in love and faithfulness. Amen.

47

CHALLENGING EACH OTHER IN FAITH

"Now faith is confidence in what we hope for and assurance about what we do not see."

— HEBREWS 11:1

One of the most powerful ways to grow together as a couple is by challenging each other to step out in faith. Faith is not just about believing; it's about trusting God enough to act on that belief, even when the path ahead isn't clear. As a couple, you have the unique opportunity to encourage and challenge each other to take bold steps of faith, both individually and together.

Challenging each other in faith begins with open conversations about your dreams, fears, and where you feel God is calling you. It's important to create a safe space where you can both express your hopes and doubts without judgment. By doing this, you can identify areas where each of you may need a gentle push to trust God more deeply or take a step that feels risky but is rooted in faith.

For instance, one of you might feel called to start a new ministry, pursue a different career path, or serve in a way that stretches your comfort zone. As partners, you can support and challenge each other by asking thoughtful questions, offering encouragement, and praying together for clarity and courage. The goal is not to push each other into decisions but to lovingly challenge each other to trust God more and to take action when He leads.

When it comes to stepping out in faith as a couple, consider setting spiritual goals that require you both to rely on God. This might mean committing to a new level of giving, volunteering for a cause that's close to your hearts, or embarking on a journey that deepens your spiritual life together. These shared challenges can strengthen your bond and help you grow closer to God as you navigate them together.

Next Steps

1. **Have Honest Conversations:** Discuss your spiritual dreams, fears, and where you feel God is leading you. Be open and supportive as you explore how you can challenge each other to step out in faith.
2. **Encourage and Pray Together:** Offer encouragement and pray together for the courage to act on what God is calling each of you to do. Prayer is a powerful way to build unity and seek God's guidance.
3. **Set Shared Faith Goals:** Identify specific goals that require both of you to trust God deeply. These could involve your personal growth, your relationship, or how you serve others together.

Real Talk

- How can we challenge each other to step out in faith, both individually and as a couple?
- What specific steps of faith do we feel called to take, and how can we support each other in taking them?

Short Prayer

Lord, thank You for the gift of faith and the opportunity to grow together in it. Help us to challenge each other with love and encouragement, so that we may step out in faith and trust You more deeply. Guide us as we seek to follow Your will, both individually and as a couple. Amen.

48

PURSUING GROWTH OPPORTUNITIES TOGETHER

"Commit to the Lord whatever you do, and he will establish your plans."

— PROVERBS 16:3

In a loving relationship, there's nothing more rewarding than seeing your partner grow and thrive in all areas of life. Whether it's spiritual, professional, or personal growth, helping each other pursue new opportunities strengthens your bond and deepens your connection. It's about being each other's biggest supporter and celebrating every milestone together.

Think about the iconic love story in *Titanic*, where Jack and Rose challenge each other to embrace new experiences and opportunities despite the obstacles. Jack encourages Rose to break free from the constraints of her life and discover her true self, while Rose inspires Jack to dream beyond his current circumstances. Their relationship becomes a catalyst for growth, helping each other reach new heights.

Similarly, in your relationship, you can inspire each other to pursue growth by being a constant source of encouragement. Whether one of you is exploring a new career path, deepening your spiritual journey, or learning a new skill, the support you provide each other can make all the difference. Start by having open conversations about your goals and dreams. Identify what each of you wants to achieve and discuss how you can help make those dreams a reality.

Beyond just encouragement, consider setting shared goals that allow you to grow together. This could involve taking a class, volunteering for a cause you both care about, or even setting spiritual practices that deepen your faith as a couple. By pursuing growth opportunities together, you not only build a stronger relationship but also create shared experiences that enrich your lives.

Next Steps

1. **Support Each Other's Dreams:** Take time to understand each other's goals and offer your full support. Encourage your partner to take steps toward their aspirations, whether it's in their career, faith, or personal life.
2. **Create Shared Goals:** Identify opportunities for growth that you can pursue together. These shared experiences will help you grow closer and create lasting memories.
3. **Celebrate Every Step:** Acknowledge and celebrate each milestone along the way. Whether big or small, every achievement is a step forward in your journey together.

Real Talk

- How can we help each other pursue new opportunities for growth, whether spiritual, professional, or personal?
- What specific steps can we take to support each other's dreams and goals?

Short Prayer

Lord, thank You for the opportunity to grow together in love and in life. Help us to support each other's dreams and to pursue new opportunities with faith and courage. Guide us as we commit our plans to You, knowing that You will establish our path. Amen.

Encouraging Each Other's Growth

Pause & Reflect

How can we better support each other's personal and spiritual growth??

Plan & Promise

What's one way we can actively encourage and nurture each other's growth this week?

Create & Connect

Choose a personal or spiritual goal that each of you wants to achieve. Write down the steps needed to reach it, and discuss how you can support each other through the process.

In encouraging each other's growth, we uplift our relationship, drawing closer to God and to each other with every step forward.

49

LESSONS LEARNED IN OUR MARRIAGE

"And we know that in all things God works for the good of those who love him, who have been called according to his purpose."

— ROMANS 8:28

Marriage is a journey filled with both joys and challenges, and along the way, we gather valuable lessons that shape who we are as a couple. These lessons are not just memories from the past; they are building blocks for the future. Reflecting on the lessons we've learned helps us carry forward the wisdom we've gained, ensuring that our relationship continues to grow stronger with time.

One of the most important lessons we've learned is the value of communication. In the early years of our marriage, misunderstandings often arose from a lack of clear and honest communication. Over time, we realized that being open with each other about our feelings, needs, and expectations is essential to maintaining a healthy relationship. Now, we prioritize regular check-ins and honest conversations, even when the topics are difficult. This commitment to communication has deepened our trust and made our connection stronger.

Another lesson we've learned is the importance of patience and grace. Marriage brings together two imperfect people, each with their own quirks and shortcomings. We've had to learn to be patient with each other's flaws and extend grace when mistakes are made. This doesn't mean ignoring issues, but rather choosing to respond with understanding and compassion. By embracing patience and grace, we've created a safe space where both of us feel loved and accepted, even when we fall short.

We've also learned the significance of shared faith. Trusting in God's plan has been a cornerstone of our marriage. Through the highs and lows, we've seen how God works all things together for our good, even when we didn't understand His purpose at the time. Leaning on our faith has given us the strength to persevere through challenges, knowing that we are not alone in our journey. This reliance on God has brought us closer to Him and to each other, grounding our marriage in something greater than ourselves.

Next Steps

1. **Prioritize Communication:** Make open and honest communication a regular practice in your marriage. It's the foundation of trust and understanding.
2. **Practice Patience and Grace:** Remember that both of you are imperfect. Choose to respond with kindness and understanding when mistakes happen.
3. **Lean on Shared Faith:** Trust in God's plan for your marriage, knowing that He is working for your good. Let your faith be the anchor that holds you together.

Real Talk

- What lessons have we learned in our marriage that we want to carry forward into the future?
- How can we apply these lessons to continue growing and strengthening our relationship?

Short Prayer

Lord, thank You for the lessons You've taught us in our marriage. Help us to carry these lessons forward with wisdom and grace, trusting that You are working all things for our good. Guide us as we continue to grow together, deepening our love for each other and our faith in You. Amen.

50

ENVISIONING OUR FUTURE TOGETHER

> *"For I know the plans I have for you,"* declares the Lord, *"plans to prosper you and not to harm you, plans to give you hope and a future."*
>
> — JEREMIAH 29:11

Envisioning your future together as a couple is one of the most meaningful ways to strengthen your relationship. It's about dreaming big, setting goals, and planning for what lies ahead, while staying grounded in the love and commitment you share. Just like in the song *Endless Love* by Lionel Richie and Diana Ross, which speaks of an enduring love that can withstand the test of time, building a shared future requires both vision and dedication.

Start by discussing your hopes and dreams. These conversations help you understand each other's desires and goals, whether related to career, family, spiritual growth, or lifestyle. Listening carefully ensures both of you feel heard and valued. Once you find common ground, you can shape a vision for your shared life.

For example, if one of you dreams of starting a family while the other is focused on career advancement, work together to create a timeline that honors both aspirations. If one of you is passionate about deepening your spiritual journey, explore ways to incorporate that into your shared life, like joining a faith-based community or setting aside time for prayer together.

Once you have a clear vision of your future, it's time to think about the practical steps needed to get there. Setting short-term and long-term goals can help make your vision a reality. These might include financial planning, setting aside time for personal development, or working on your relationship through regular check-ins and communication. It's also helpful to revisit these goals periodically, adjusting them as needed to reflect any changes in your circumstances or priorities. This ensures that you stay aligned as a couple and continue moving forward together.

One of the key elements to successfully working toward your shared future is staying committed to the process. It's easy to get caught up in the daily grind and lose sight of your bigger dreams, but by regularly reminding each other of your shared goals, you can stay focused and motivated. Make it a habit to encourage each other, celebrate the small wins along the way, and stay supportive even when challenges arise. Remember, the journey towards your future is as important as the destination itself.

Next Steps

1. **Dream and Share:** Take time to share individual and shared goals to build a future that reflects both your desires.
2. **Plan with Purpose:** Set practical goals, whether saving for a home, planning for a family, or deepening your spiritual life.
3. **Stay Encouraged:** Keep each other motivated by discussing progress, celebrating successes, and staying committed to shared goals.

Real Talk

- How do we envision our future together, and what steps can we take now to work towards it?
- What are some specific goals we can set today to help us achieve the future we desire?

Short Prayer

Lord, thank You for the future You have planned for us. Help us dream together with faith and love, and guide us as we build a life that honors You. Amen.

51

APPLYING GOD'S WISDOM IN OUR MARRIAGE

"If any of you lacks wisdom, you should ask God, who gives generously to all without finding fault, and it will be given to you."

— JAMES 1:5

Marriage is a journey filled with lessons, many of which come directly from God's wisdom. Through the ups and downs, God teaches us about patience, love, forgiveness, and the importance of putting Him at the center of our relationship. Reflecting on what God has taught us through our marriage helps us apply His wisdom as we move forward, strengthening our bond and deepening our faith.

One of the key lessons God has taught me is the value of humility and selflessness. In the early days of our marriage, I often found myself focused on my own needs and expectations. Over time, God showed me that marriage is not just about what I can receive, but about what I can give. By learning to put my spouse's needs above my own and serving with a humble heart, I've experienced the true joy that comes from loving selflessly, just as Christ loves us.

God has also taught me the importance of seeking His guidance in every aspect of our marriage. There have been times when we faced difficult decisions or challenges that seemed overwhelming. In those moments, turning to God in prayer and asking for His wisdom has brought clarity and peace. God's guidance has shown us the right path, even when it wasn't the easiest one. By trusting in

His plan, we've been able to navigate challenges with confidence, knowing that He is always with us.

Forgiveness is another powerful lesson God has instilled in our marriage. No relationship is perfect, and there are times when we hurt each other, whether intentionally or unintentionally. Through God's example of grace and forgiveness, I've learned that holding onto grudges only creates distance. Instead, choosing to forgive quickly and completely allows us to heal and grow closer together. God's wisdom reminds us that forgiveness is not just an act of letting go, but a way of reflecting His love in our relationship.

As we continue our journey together, I'm committed to applying the wisdom God has given us. This means staying humble, seeking His guidance, and practicing forgiveness daily. It also means continually asking God for wisdom, knowing that He is generous in providing it when we need it most. With God's wisdom as our foundation, I believe our marriage will continue to thrive, growing stronger with each passing day.

Next Steps

1. **Practice Humility:** Serve your spouse selflessly, prioritizing their needs and showing love in practical ways.
2. **Seek God's Guidance:** Make prayer a regular part of your decision-making process. Trust that His wisdom will guide you.
3. **Embrace Forgiveness:** Let go of past hurts quickly. Forgiveness allows your marriage to heal and grow.

Real Talk

- What has God taught us through our marriage, and how can we apply that wisdom moving forward?
- How can we continue to seek God's guidance and apply His wisdom in our daily lives as a couple?

Short Prayer

Lord, thank You for the wisdom You've given us through our marriage. Help us apply it as we grow together. Teach us to love selflessly, seek Your guidance, and forgive as You forgive us. May Your wisdom guide our relationship in all we do. Amen.

52

KEEPING GOD AT THE CENTER OF OUR PLANS

"But seek first his kingdom and his righteousness, and all these things will be given to you as well."

— MATTHEW 6:33

When planning for the future, it's easy for couples to focus on practical concerns like finances, career goals, or family decisions. However, the most important element to consider is ensuring that God remains at the center of those plans. By seeking His guidance and prioritizing His will above all else, couples can build a future that is not only successful but also aligned with God's purpose for their lives.

To keep God at the center of their plans, couples should begin by committing every decision to prayer. Before making major decisions—whether it's buying a home, changing jobs, or starting a family—taking time to seek God's direction ensures that they are walking in His will. This can be done by praying together regularly, asking for wisdom, and waiting on God's timing. When couples make God's guidance their priority, they can trust that He will lead them on the right path.

In addition to prayer, studying Scripture together can help couples keep their focus on God's priorities. By reflecting on verses that emphasize trust, faith, and obedience, couples can remind themselves of what truly matters. For example, Matthew 6:33 serves as a powerful reminder that when they seek God's kingdom first, everything else will fall into place. This scripture can be a guiding principle for the coming year, encouraging them to prioritize their spiritual growth and reliance on God above all else.

Moreover, couples can set spiritual goals that align with their plans for the future. These might include committing to serve in their church, engaging in regular Bible study, or finding ways to support each other's spiritual growth. By setting goals that honor God, they ensure that their relationship and future plans are built on a solid foundation of faith.

Next Steps

1. **Commit to Prayer:** Make it a habit to pray together about your future plans. Seek God's guidance in every decision, trusting that He will lead you according to His will.
2. **Study Scripture Together:** Reflect on key Bible verses that emphasize seeking God's kingdom first. Let these scriptures guide your decisions and remind you to prioritize your spiritual growth.
3. **Set Spiritual Goals:** Establish goals that help you keep God at the center of your lives. Whether it's serving together, studying the Bible, or supporting each other's faith journey, these goals will help you stay focused on what truly matters.

Real Talk

- How can we keep God at the center of our future plans, and what specific steps can we take to prioritize His will?
- What scripture will guide us in the coming year as we seek to align our plans with God's purpose?

Short Prayer

Lord, thank You for being our guide and our source of wisdom. Help us to keep You at the center of all our plans, trusting in Your perfect timing and direction. As we look to the future, may we seek Your kingdom first, knowing that when we do, You will provide for all our needs. Lead us, Lord, and help us to walk in Your will every step of the way. Amen.

Reflecting on the Past & Looking Ahead

Pause & Reflect

What lessons have we learned in our marriage, and how can we carry those lessons into the future?

Plan & Promise

What's one step we can take this week to begin planning for our future, while applying the lessons we've learned?

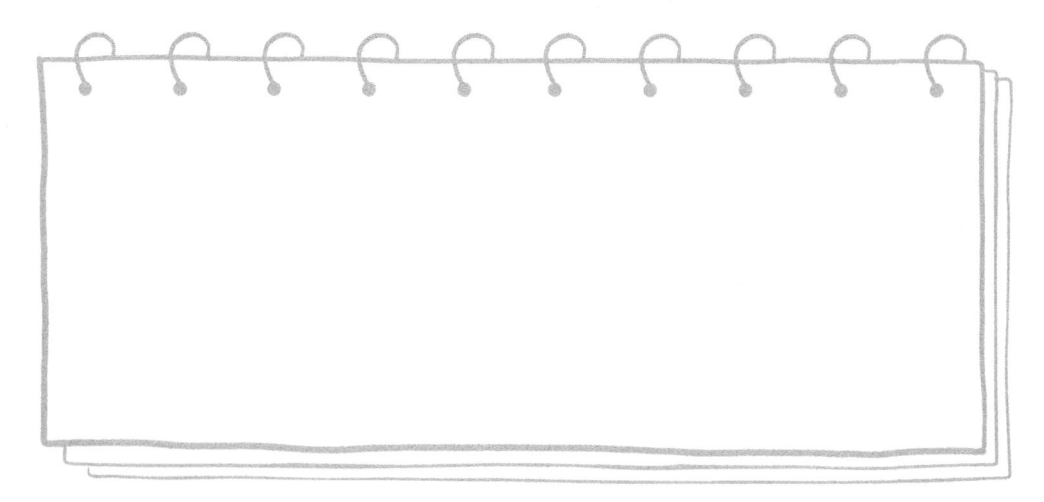

Create & Connect

Write letters to each other reflecting on the most valuable lessons you've learned throughout your relationship.

Reflecting on our past, we see the lessons that have shaped us. Looking ahead, we embrace the future with faith, love, and a shared commitment to growth."

KEEPING YOUR LOVE STORY ALIVE

"Let us consider how we may spur one another on toward love and good deeds."

— HEBREWS 10:24

Now that you've completed this devotional, you and your spouse have deepened your connection through faith, love, and intentional growth. It's time to pass on the blessings by sharing your experience with others. By leaving an honest review of this book on Amazon, you'll help other couples find the same strength, wisdom, and encouragement in their relationship.

Your review will provide valuable insights for couples looking for guidance on how to strengthen their bond through faith. By sharing your journey, you'll be helping others discover the peace, joy, and unity that comes from focusing on God together.

Thank you for your help. Marriage is enriched when we share our experiences and encourage one another—and you're playing a part in that!

Scan below to leave your review on Amazon:

Your review is a testament to the power of faith in marriage and a guiding light for couples seeking deeper connection. Thank you for being part of this community and for helping others build lasting relationships grounded in God's love.

With gratitude,

Biblical Teachings

CONTINUING TOGETHER

Congratulations on embarking on the lifelong journey of marriage. Whether you're newlyweds learning to navigate life together or seasoned partners deepening your bond, this season brings growth, love, and connection. May your hearts be filled with gratitude for the love you share and hope for the future God has planned for you both.

Marriage is a beautiful journey with its own challenges and blessings. The joy—the laughter, shared dreams, and love—is woven with difficulty. Through it all, God is with you, guiding your steps and strengthening your relationship.

This devotional is here to help you grow as a couple, reminding you that your relationship is built on love, patience, and faith. Through the stories of biblical couples and reflections, we encourage you to nurture your bond and trust God's hand in your marriage.

Each day offers a chance to deepen your connection. Kind words, gentle touches, and shared prayers can strengthen your relationship in profound ways. Continue to prioritize each other, and let God's presence guide you.

Thank you for allowing this devotional to join you on your journey of love and faith. May it remind you of God's unwavering love and the joy of a marriage centered on Him. Keep seeking His guidance, and may your future together be filled with grace, peace, and countless blessings.

With love and prayers,

Biblical Teachings

Made in the USA
Middletown, DE
20 September 2025